Foreword

Sir David Hanson

The conflict that came to be known as the Great War, and later the First World War changed the world for ever and impacted upon the lives of millions of people across nations.

Throughout the world lives were destroyed, communities upended and sadly, the seeds for future conflicts were planted.

The bravery of a generation was put to the test but in towns across the UK such as Holywell, those immense events were seen in a different way, through the lens of local loss and local tragedy.

This book tells the story of those Holywell men for whom that war meant the ultimate sacrifice - the men of Holywell who gave their lives in War and who now have immortality through commemoration on the Holywell War Memorial.

This book will show they were more than just names on a memorial - they were Sons, Husbands, Brothers and Friends, Uncles, Neighbours and Sweet-hearts.

They walked the same streets as we do today and would recognise buildings we see in the town now. They held down jobs, played sports and had dreams for the future. Dreams that would perish with them on the field of conflict.

This book will tell their story - who they were, how they lived and how they died.

As time has gone on, that history has been forgotten by many, but not by the author of this book Russ Warburton.

That's why I very much welcome this book, as Russ helps tell the stories of those men and helps keep their memories alive today.

I know Russ will agree that it's been a labour of love.

Russ, like myself, had a Grandfather who fought in that war.

Like my Grandfather, his came home, lived, loved and created a life.

It is fitting that for those who did not return, their lives are now remembered.

My congratulation goes to Russ for this herculean effort over 5 years to bring these stories together. In writing this book he does a service, not just to the town, but to the memories of those the town lost.

Please read it and remember the lives these men lived and the future potential that Holywell lost. It is a story of bravery and sacrifice that needs to be told.

Rt. hon Sir David Hanson

Member of parliament for Delyn 1992-2019

Copyright © 2020 Russ Warburton.
All rights reserved.
Cover design by Karen Humphreys
Book design by Russ Warburton
No part of this book can be reproduced in any form
or by written, electronic or mechanical, including
photocopying, recording, or by any information
retrieval system without written permission
in writing by the author.

Although every precaution has been taken in
the preparation of this book, the publisher
and author assume no responsibility for
errors or omissions. Neither is any liability
assumed for damages resulting from the
use of information contained herein.

Preface

In the 21st century, the terrible Wars of the 20th century seem remote, belonging to a bygone era, there are no Veterans of the First World War still alive, Veterans from the Second World War are slowly fading away, many of us buy a Poppy during November and observe a 2 minute silence for the fallen, although most of us knew neither the soldiers, nor their times, we might look at the list of faceless names on the local war memorials as we hurry by, but they are just names to us now and old fashioned ones at that, I wonder how long our respect for them will continue?

Having always had a keen interest in the History of the First and Second World Wars, reading many books on the subject and visiting the former battlefields of France and Belgium many times, I decided to trace my Taid's (Welsh name for Grandfather) Service War Record.

My Taid died in 1969 when I was 8 years old. I remember him telling me and my Brother Steve, that he was wounded in the First World War, we paid little attention to his stories, as he was 90 and we were, sadly, more interested in annoying him. 50 years later I have traced his record and visited where he served in Belgium. Luckily, my Taid survived the War and returned home, while many were not so lucky, I turned my attention to the men on my local War Memorial on the old Town Hall, Holywell, who fought with my Taid, and paid the ultimate sacrifice. Who were they? How old were they? Where did they live and work? What life did they have before the War? Where was their final resting place? So, this is their stories. I am not a Historian; I have tried to put together as much information as I could find. I hope you find their stories of interest.

Next time you walk past the Memorial, in the High Street, please pause for a minute and remember the boys (yes some were boys) and men who gave their lives for the sake of their family, town and country.

I hope, we will always remember them.

Acknowledgements

This book could not have been written without the help of the following: -

Flintshire War Memorials Project

Chris Baker and his website "The Long Long Trail"

The Great War Forum, for the help in gathering information

The staff of the Hawarden Record Office, for their help and patience in dealing with a novice

The relatives of the men listed on the Holywell Memorial

Steve and Lizzie, Lin and Karl, my Brother, Sister and Partners, for their support

To Steph and Kev, my Daughter and Son, so proud of both of you

To Christopher, Jack and Georgia, my "other" children, so proud of you all

To the following members of "Pot Luck Tours", how we ever found any of the places in France and Belgium, is still a mystery to me, but thank you for some fantastic times. Steve Warburton, Kevin Warburton, Stevie Warburton, Stuart Howson, David Bamford, Graham Renshaw, David Renshaw, Nigel Tudor, Karl Lurz, Peter Selley

And finally, to Karen, my Partner, for all of your encouragement given to complete this book and for typing it all up and putting into some semblance of order and also for just being my girl and making me so happy in life.

Dedication

This book is dedicated to my wonderful Grandchildren, from a very proud Taid

Mia Grace Warburton

Lexi Neve Warburton

Lucie Summer Bamford

Harry David Bamford

May you always be happy in life

Contents

Chapter 1 ..... Call to Arms

Chapter 2..... The Holywell First World War Memorial

Chapter 3.....Roll of Honour, The Men on the Holywell Memorial (Part 1 & 2)

Chapter 4.... The Battalions in which they Served

Chapter 5,,,,, Evacuation of the Wounded

Chapter 6..... The Missing

Chapter 7..... Burying the Fallen in WW1

Chapter 8..... The Home Front

Chapter 9..... Coming Home

Chapter 10..... My Taid – Edwin Roberts

Chapter 11.... Dig Hill 80 – Finding the Fallen

Chapter 12.....List of Men who Served from Holywell

Chapter 1
Call to Arms

The "Call to Arms", in and around the Holywell area, was the same as across the whole of the Country, Everyone, it seems, were keen to "*do their bit*", many joining up very quickly, just in case they missed out, as rumour was that the war would be over by Christmas and the British Empire would prevail in the fight against the evil aggressor. Recruiting drives and numerous meetings were held in and around Holywell.

An example of these meetings was held in the Local Assembly Hall, an article appeared in The County Herald on 11th September 1914 entitled: -

"Holywell and the War, an enthusiastic Meeting"

There was a crowded attendance at the Assembly Hall on the Tuesday evening when a meeting was held for the purpose of inducting the men of the district to join Lord Kitchener's Army. The Chair was occupied by Hon-Major J. Lloyd Price, who was supported on the platform by Col. Howard, the Vicar J. W. Thomas, Dr. H. W. S. Williams, Alderman Joseph Jones, Messer D. F. Pennant, H. A. Tilby (Clerk of Flintshire County Council), Thomas Waterhouse, Captain James Ayer, J. Kerfoot Roberts, Frank Jones, Rhyl.

In the course of the opening remarks, The Chairman, alluded to the valiant manner in which the British Army was fighting in France and stated nothing like it had ever been recorded in history, but the Army wanted reinforcements and "Where were they to come from?" It was for the young able-bodied men of the country, to come to their assistance, because it would be a shame to leave them alone to fight their Country's Battles in France *(hear, hear)*. He had hoped Lord Mostyn would have been able to attend this meeting, but he was not well enough to do so. He referred to the ex-Officer of that district Mr Ayer, who had done excellent work, proving himself one of the best in the Country in recruiting and sent an excellent lot of men to Wrexham and Chester. Colonel Howard then addressed the meeting. He said that the recent performance of the British army was the most remarkable military feat ever recorded in history *(hear, hear)*, they had beaten the Germans who were five to one against them *(applause)*, but General French had sent home to say, he must have more men in order to maintain their position in the field and in Europe, and to the men of Holywell, he *(The Speaker)* appealed that night, Lord Kitchener has asked for 500,000 more men and had already 300,000, so 200,000 were still required.

These new troops would be put into training as soon as possible and as soon as the Inspecting Officer was satisfied as to their fitness, they would be sent to the Front, and not before. During the past few days, he had been with his friend, Mr Herbert Lewis, speaking at meetings of this character *(hear, hear)* there was no distinction of politics now. They all stood on one common platform *(hear, hear)*.

The Speaker then referred to the numbers raised in Flintshire at the time of the Napoleonic Wars and said at that time, the loyal Holywell volunteers, were 140 strong *(hear, hear)*. Proceeding to refer to the prospects of the great struggle, Colonel Howard described what would happen if Germany won. They had, he said, to deal with a powerful and unscrupulous enemy, and they wanted to be in a position to deal with him in such a way, as to crush his power forever *(hear, hear)*. War was Hell, there is no other word for it. Lord Kitchener's objective, in raising his new Army, was to keep the War out of this Country. He appealed to the young men of the good old Town of Holywell, to come forward, your men between the ages of 19-35, should do their duty to their Country, which was in such terrible danger at the present moment.

Mr H. A. Tilby then delivered a forceful and inspiring address. He said that if Britain were beaten in this fight, they would have to abandon all those high ideals of freedom and liberty for which they now stood, and they would be governed by brute force, might against right. He hoped and believed they were going to win, but that would have to come by fighting, not by shouting *(hear, hear)*. They wanted to show by their deeds, that they had men who were determined. Their ideals should continue to live. He appealed to the young men, if they wanted to end it, this is the way to stop the awful devastation and to roll up and roll up at once, to go and fight side by side, shoulder to shoulder, with those who were upholding the Flag of this Country so valiantly at the front *(hear, hear)*.

James Ayer was the main Recruiting Officer for the district and enthusiastically went about his work. His only Son, Leonard Stuart Ayer, joined up and was sadly later killed in the action in 1916. (see 13th RWF).

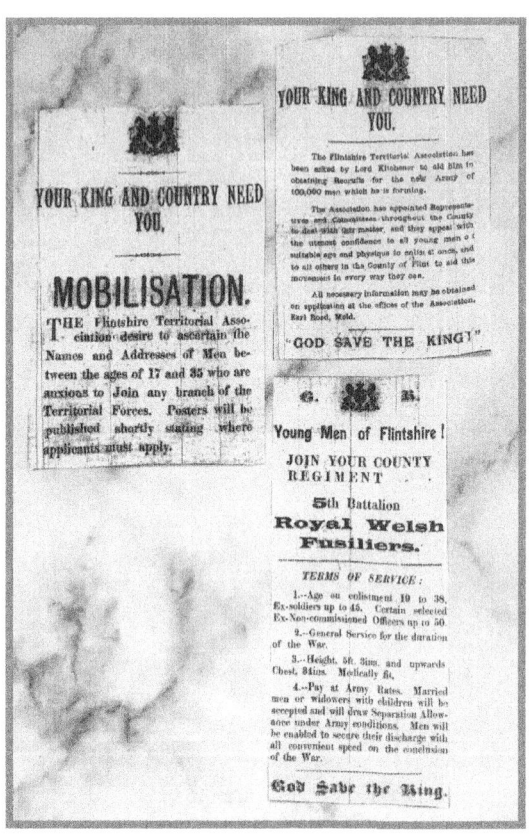

Adverts that appeared in the Local County Herald Newspaper. 7th August 1914, 14th August 1914. March 12th 1915

Drill Hall Halkyn Street Holywell

The Drill Hall was built in 1914 by John Sibeon & Sons of Holywell, replacing the Drill Hall in Brynford Street, which had been home to the Yeomanry.

*Authors own photograph

Chapter 2
The Holywell First World War Memorial

The two slabs of grey granite on the frontage of the old Town Hall, each bearing sixteen names of the men from Holywell, who made the ultimate sacrifice.

The plaques were made by Samuel Walsby of Liverpool at a cost of £130.00. The money was raised by the general public.

The parade was not a military one but was made up of the men from Holywell who had served during the War, who were the lucky ones to return home.

The parade left from the Drill Hall in Halkyn Street and were under command of Major Elford H. Roberts, to form a square in front of the Town Hall. A small platform was built in front of the Town Hall; the ceremony was very well attended by the locals.

The ceremony was presided over by Horace Waterhouse, Chairman of Holywell District Council. He was accompanied by Rev. E Lorimer Thomas, Father Ryan, Doctor Oliver, Lt. Col. T. H. Parry D. S. O. MP, Mr W. Buckley High Sheriff of Flintshire, and Mr Kerfoot Roberts Clerk to Holywell Urban District Council.

The ceremony opened with the singing of "O Freneau Caersalem" (Kings of Jerusalem). Doctor Oliver, followed with reading a lesson. Mr Waterhouse gave a short address stating that during 1914-1918 between five and six hundred men from Holywell had joined His Majesty's Forces and thankfully the majority had returned. Mr Waterhouse said that this was a Memorial to the brave and gallant men, whose names were placed in the façade of the Town Hall, could be remembered by all who passed by and made tribute to those who gave so much in a great cause. After a further reading, they called upon John Williams to unveil the plaques. John Williams lived with his Parents at 1 St. Winifred's Terrace, he had two Brothers, Mesech and William, both killed. Mesech killed in 1916, William killed in 1918. John, himself, was severely injured during the conflict, all three had served in the R.W.F and he had been selected to perform the ceremony, many people agreeing that no one else was more worthy of the honour.

After unveiling the plaques, Father Ryan offered a dedicatory Prayer, which was followed by The Lord's Prayer.

Lt. Col. Parry gave an address to the assembled in which he said that in all the horror of the War, perhaps the greatest word that had come from it was "Comradeship". The ceremony concluded with the singing of the hymn "On the Resurrection Morning" followed by the Last Post and the laying of four wreaths, including one by Mrs Lawton Denton, in memory of her Son killed in 1917, Captain James Ayer also laid a wreath in memory of his only Son Captain Leonard S. Ayer killed in 1916.

The parade, reformed of ex-servicemen, marched in column to the Drill Hall in Halkyn Street to the sound of a drummer boy's beat.

The Unveiling of the Roll of Honour Memorial Holywell Town Hall

Former Soldiers on parade outside the Roll of Honour Memorial Holywell

Marching past the Hotel Victoria towards the Town Hall

*A video is available to watch the Holywell Memorial unveiling at: -

https://player.bfi.org.uk/free/film/watch-unveiling-of-1914-1918-war-roll-of-honour-at-holywell-c-1919-1919-online

Chapter 3
Roll of Honour - The Men on the Holywell Memorial
Part 1

Private 238168 Herbert Edward Abbott
13th Battalion Royal Welsh Fusiliers
5th Battalion Royal Welsh Fusiliers
(Boy Soldier 1462)

Herbert Edward Abbott was born on 30th October 1899 in Liverpool. His Parents were Herbert Edward and Alice Ann Abbott.

During the 1900, the family moved from Liverpool to Rhyl and lived as boarders at the back of 54 Wellington Road.

His Father, Herbert, was aged 27 and employed as a Boot Maker. His Wife, Alice, was aged 26 and their Son Herbert Edward Abbott, aged 1 year. Also living with them at this time was Herbert's Sister Nellie Abbott aged 17.

On August 3rd 1903, the family moved from Rhyl to live at Summer Hill, Brynford Street, Holywell.

The 1911 census shows Alice Ann Abbott as an inmate at the Holywell Workhouse (Lluesty Hospital as it is known today), while her Children, Herbert Edward Abbott, aged 11, John William Abbott, aged 10 and Louisa Gertrude Abbott, aged 7, were all residents of a Children's Home which was known as Cottage House Holywell and was situated very near to the Workhouse.

There is no trace of the Father, Herbert senior, at this time, it is not known whether he had died, deserted his family, or still living in Holywell. On the Workhouse register, Alice Ann refers to herself as married and not a widow.

Eventually, Alice Ann and her Children were reunited and returned to live at Summer Hill, Brynford Street, Holywell.

When Herbert reached the age of 13, he obtained employment as a trainee Spinner at the Welsh Flannel Mill, Greenfield Road, Holywell, to help with the family finances.

On Wednesday 5th August 1914, at the outbreak of the First World War, Herbert was recorded as being embodied into the 5th Battalion Royal Welsh Fusiliers as a Boy Soldier. On the 15th of April 1915 he was admitted to a Military Hospital suffering from pneumonia. He was a patient in the hospital for 3 months, being discharged 23rd July 1915 and returned to his unit.

He transferred to the 13th Battalion Royal Welsh Fusiliers as a Front-Line Soldier and fought mainly in the Battles of the Hindenburg Line, Battle of Albert, Battle of Cambrai before being severely wounded during the Battle of Epehy. He died of his wounds received in action on 16th September 1918, aged 19, while in hospital in Rouen. He was buried in St. Sever Cemetery Extension, Rouen. His personal effects consisted of a metal cigarette case with a brown clasp, letters, metal ring, purse with a clip badge containing a few coins, book wallet, photographs, postcard, and a note book. They were forwarded to his Mother at 2 Summer Hill.

Herbert is also remembered on the North Wales Heroes' Memorial Arch, Bangor.

Private Herbert Edward Abbott is buried at St. Sever Extension Cemetery. Plot 11 - Row K - Grave 14 - Rouen Seine - Maritime - France

Plaque on St James's Parish Church wall Holywell

Herbert is also remembered on the North Wales Heroes' Memorial Arch in Bangor

- To read more details on the Battalion that Herbert served with see 5th Battalion/13th Battalion Royal Welsh Fusiliers – in Chapter 4 of this book

Captain Leonard Stuart Ayer
13th Battalion Royal Welsh Fusiliers

Leonard Stuart Ayer was born in Holywell Flintshire in July 1891.

The 1901 census shows the family living in Holywell, Flintshire, Head of the family was James Ayer aged 34, a Draper, his Wife Elizabeth was aged 36, Leonard Stuart, aged 10 and Agnes Eustice aged 27 a Domestic Servant.

The 1911 census states that the family resided at Victoria House, 4 Victoria Square, Holywell. The head of the family was James Ayer, aged 44, a Draper, his Wife Elizabeth aged 47, a Millinery Buyer and their Son Leonard Stuart, a Bank Clerk, employed by London City & Midland Bank, Holywell. There was also a Domestic Servant, Miss Sarah Redfern aged 35 of Halkyn, living in the house.

James Ayer was well respected in the Holywell area and was a prominent member of the Baskingwerk Masonic Lodge, Coleshill Street Holywell. Leonard Stuart Ayer married Alice Chapman at Holywell Parish Church on 11th July 1914 and lived at The Cottage, Strand, Holywell.

Leonard Stuart Ayer was commissioned into the 13th Battalion Royal Welsh Fusiliers on the 12th of October 1914. At the age of 23 years, his height was stated at 6ft. The Recruiting Officer at the time of his enlistment was his Father James Ayer.

Leonard Stuart previously served with the Scottish Battalion the Kings Liverpool for 2 years 144 days. He was Lieutenant and then promoted to Captain on the 19th of May 1916. Leonard Stuart Ayer died of his wounds he received in the Battle of Mametz Wood on the 15th of July 1916 at Heilly Hospital Aid Station Mericourt, L'Abbe. His Wife Alice was sent a telegram dated 16.07.1916 informing her that her Husband had been wounded and further news would follow. The telegram was dated one day after Leonard Stuart had died of his wounds. Alice received no further news of Leonard Stuart, so on the 9th of August she sent a letter through to her Solicitor asking for more news of her Husband's condition. The Army replied informing Alice of the sad news.

Leonard Stuart Ayer's personal effects were returned to Alice which were listed as follows: -

- 1 cheque book
- 1 cheque book (Cox & Co)
- 1 identity disc
- 1 Franc (souvenir)
- 1 notecase
- 1 wristwatch
- 1 handkerchief
- 1 whistle
- 1 scale
- 2 badges
- 9 buttons
- 1 pair of gloves
- 1 wrist disc with charm attached

Leonard Stuart Ayer is buried at Heilly Station Cemetery.

His Father James died in 1943 aged 66. His Mother Elizabeth died in 1947 aged 74.

They, like many others, never got to see their only Son's grave.

At the time of writing this book, I owned a Business/Shop in Holywell High Street and with Leonards Stuart Ayer's family owing a Business/Shop in Holywell too, we thought it would be a poignant gesture to visit his grave, from one Business Owner to another.

My Partner Karen and I made a pilgrimage to Heilly Station Cemetery in August 2016 to visit Leonard Stuart Ayers grave and to show that he, like all others who made the ultimate sacrifice, was not forgotten.

*Authors own photograph

Captain Leonard Stuart Ayer & his grave at Heilly Station Cemetery

Captain Leonard Stuart Ayer – 13th Battalion Royal Welsh Fusiliers

Back Row 2nd from the Left

The Train Station at Heilly   *Authors own photograph

This is where the wounded, including Ayer, would have been transported to, from the front.

The road leading to the 36th Casualty Clearing Station

This is where the wounded Ayer would have been treated

*Authors own photographs

A Telegram dated 16.07.1916 informing Alice Ayer, his Wife, that her Husband was wounded 10th July 1916 and further information would follow

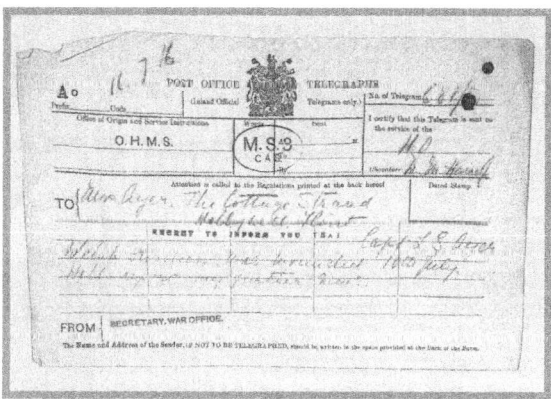

A letter from Ayers family's Solicitors asking for more information on Leonard's condition dated 9th August 1916

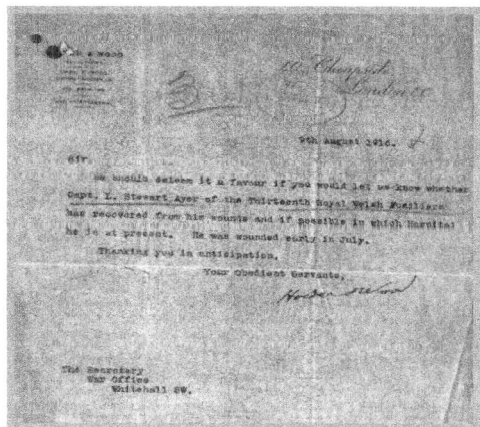

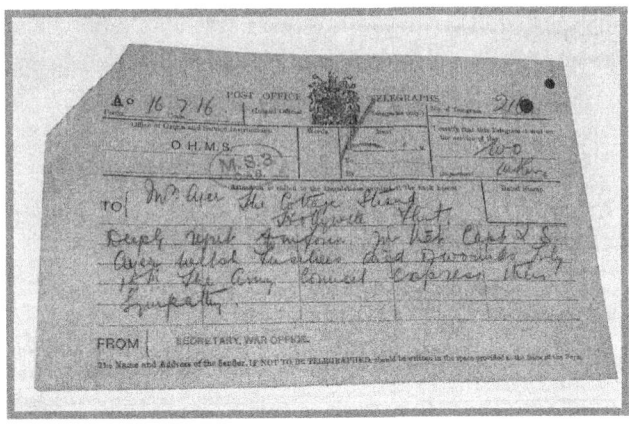

A copy of the Telegram also dated 16.07.1916 informing Alice that her Husband, has died of his wounds. It's obvious, Alice never received this Telegram

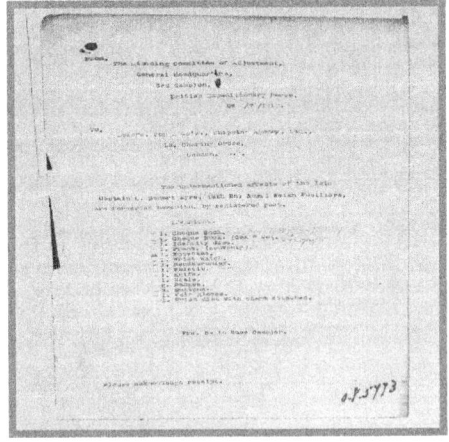

List of personal effects that were returned to Leonard Stuart Ayers Wife Alice Ann

Midland Bank Memorial in London

For all Midland Bank workers who were killed in First World War

The HSBC (previously The Midland Bank), Holywell High Street,

Where Leonard Stuart Ayer worked before signing up

- To read more details on the Battalion that Leonard served with see 13th Battalion Royal Welsh Fusiliers – in Chapter 4 of this book

Private 54605 (10380) John Boyes
2nd Battalion Royal Welsh Fusiliers

John Boyes was born in Holywell December 1897 and was baptised on 9th January 1898 at Holywell Parish Church. At the time, the family resided at "Back Cain Holywell."

The 1911 census states that the family had now moved to 4 Davies's Square, New Road, Holywell. The Head of the family was Stephen a 42, Coal Heaver (unloading coal carts in the mines) who was born in St. Helens Lancashire. His Wife Sarah Elizabeth aged 41, their 3 Children Robert aged 15, John aged 14 and Hanna Jane aged 10.

John was killed in action Wednesday 7th March 1917 and is buried at Peronne Communal Cemetery Extension France. Plot III – Row J – Grave 31.

He is also remembered on the North Wales Heroes' Memorial Arch in Bangor.

- **To read more details on the Battalion that John served with see 2nd Battalion Royal Welsh Fusiliers – in Chapter 4 of this book**

Peronne Communal Cemetery Extension, France

Plot III - Row J - Grave 31

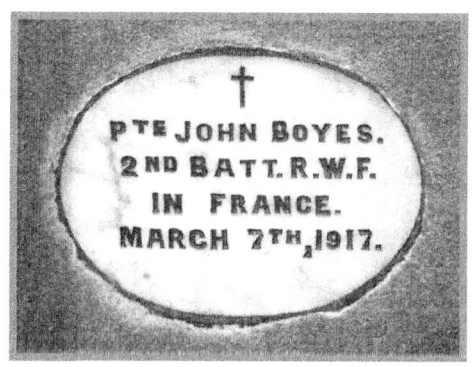

Plaque on St James's Parish Church wall Holywell

John is also remembered on the North Wales Heroes' Memorial Arch in Bangor

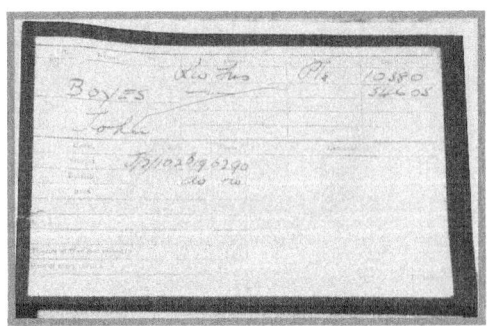

Private John Boyes Medal Card

Private John James Conlon 67092 R.A.M.C.
Royal Army Medical Corps

John James Conlon was born in Holywell in 1890.

The 1911 census states that he lived with his family residing at 16 Primrose Hill, Holywell. The Head of the family was John Henry Conlon aged 48, a General Labourer, his Wife Ann Conlon aged 44 and their 8 Children. Thomas aged 23 a House Painter, John aged 21, Anthony aged 17, Frank aged 16 all employed as General Labourers, Robert 13, Joseph 10, Annie 6, Maggie 2.

John enlisted as a Private in the R.A.M.C. on 30th August 1915 in Sheffield. He is described as 5ft 6" with a 36" chest measurements with a 2" expansion. His physical development is described as good. At the time of enlistment, he lived at 32 Dodge Street, Liverpool and was employed as a Groom.

John arrived in France with the Battalion on the 9th of November 1915 and saw action there before embarkation for the Middle East on the 4th of April 1918.

Whilst on leave from the Front in France, he married Constance Mabel Wood in Leicester on August 8th 1917.

On 21st September 1918 he was admitted to hospital suffering from pneumonia and died there on the 27th of October 1918.

John James Conlon died at the Armenian Hospital Allepo, Syria on 27th October 1918 aged 29 years. He is buried at the Beirut War Cemetery, Grave 289.

I kneel behind the soldier's trench

I walk mid shambles, smear and stench

The dead I mourn

I bear the stretcher and I bend

O'er Fritz and Pierre and Jack to mend

What shells have torn   ………………………………….by John Finley

- To read more details on the R.A.M.C that John served with, see Chapter 4 of this book

Beirut War Cemetery -   Grave 289

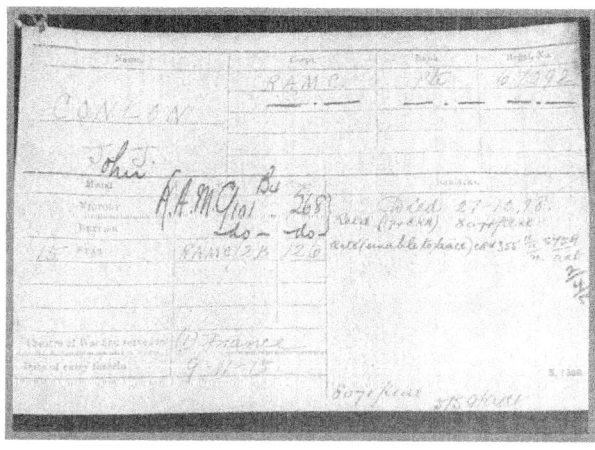

Private John James Conlon's Medal Card

Private John James Conlon's Short Service Record

Private David Owen Darley Davies 37611
15th Battalion Royal Welsh Fusiliers

David Owen Darley Davies was born in Llanidloes Montgomeryshire 6th February 1897.

The family moved to Holywell during 1909 and resided at Wesley House, Llanasa, Holywell.

The 1911 census tells us that the Head of the family was David Darley Davies aged 50, a Wesleyan Methodist Minister, his Wife Mary Ellen Darley Davies aged 40 and their Daughter Helen Myfanwy Darley Davies aged 9. David Owen Darley Davies was at that time, attending the Kingswood Wesleyan Public School, Lansdown Road, Bath and does not appear on the 1911 census at this address.

David left school aged 17 and began his employment as a Bank Clerk with the London City & Midland Bank at the Flint Branch on 6th December 1915 aged 18 years. He enlisted at Flint as a Private with the Royal Welsh Fusiliers. On enlistment he is described as 5ft 7" tall, chest measurement 34" with extension of 3", physical development good and fit for Military Service.

He embarked for France at Southampton on Monday 11th December 1916 and later posted to Ypres Belgium, where he was killed in action on Friday 27th July 1917. He is remembered on the Menin Gate panel 22 & the Midland Bank Memorial in London, for all Midland Bank workers who were killed in First World War

- To read more details about where David Owen Darley Davies' served, in the 15th Battalion Royal Welsh Fusiliers see Chapter 4 of this book

The Kingswood Wesleyan Public School in Bath

Private David Owen Darley Davies is remembered on The Menin

Gate Panel 22

Transcript of the above letter written by David's Father the Military Authorities

REF NO 12586/37611 - Wesley House Holywell

18th August 1917

Dear Sir, In reply to yours of the 14th, I beg to say that I have received as reply to a wire, from the headquarters of the Battalion, that my boy was killed on 28th July, and he was buried in the British Cemetery near Ypres. I shall be glad

1. To know that his death has been recorded by the War Office
2. Also, will you kindly know how his grave may be

Private John E. Davies 53939
1st Battalion Royal Welsh Fusiliers

Private John Edward Davies was born in 1898 and lived at 6 Dolphin Cottages, Holywell. He was the only Son of Hugh and Annie Davies. He died of his wounds aged 21 on 22nd November 1918, 11 days after the end of the War. He is buried at Montecchio Precalcino Communal Cemetery Extension in Italy.

In the 1911 census it stated that the Head of the family was Hugh Davies aged 38, a Smelter by trade and worked in the Greenfield Iron Foundry. His Wife Annie Davies was also 38, John was their only Son and was 13 at the time of the census.

He was with the 1st Battalion on Wednesday 23rd October 1918 when they tried to cross the river Piave using the Cozensa crossing, the Battalion was heavily shelled, and machine gunned, and it was during this battle that John was wounded and died later of the wounds received.

- To read more details on the Battalion John Edward Davies served, the 1st Battalion Royal Welsh Fusiliers see Chapter 4 of this book

Montecchio Precalcino Communal Cemetery, Italy

St. James Parish Church, Holywell where the plaque for John Edward Davies is situated on the wall

PTE J.E. DAVIES
1/5. R.W.F.
NOV. 22ND 1918.
IN ITALY.

Corporal Robert Thomas Davies 36413

Pembroke Yeomanry Battalion – Household Cavalry of the Line

Robert Thomas Davies was born in Holywell, February 1885 at Farm House, Holywell.

The 1911 census shows that the family now resided at 1 Summer Hill, Brynford, Holywell. The Head of the family was Mary Ann Davies a 35-year-old widow; her Husband William had died some years earlier. Mary was employed as a Charwoman at this time. Mary's only Son, Robert, aged 16 was working as a Labourer in the Welsh Flannel Mill, Greenfield Road, Holywell. She also had 3 Daughters, Margaret Jane Davies aged 14 years, Dylis Davies aged 11 and Miriam Davies aged 7.

Robert died of his wounds on Sunday 24th November 1918 aged 24.

His inscription on his gravestone says - *"He lived to die, he died to rise, the God accepted sacrifice"*

Robert is also remembered on the North Wales Heroes' Memorial Arch in Bangor

Buried in St. Peter's Church, Holywell - Gravestone is a Bodelwyddan Church

- **To read more details on the Battalion Robert Thomas Davies' served with, the Pembroke Yeomanry Battalion see Chapter 4 of this book**

Robert Thomas Davies' headstone placed within the grounds of St. Peter's Parish Church Holywell, he is in an unmarked Grave on the East side of the church

Plaque on St. James' Parish Church wall, Holywell

Headstone at St. Margaret's Church, Bodelwyddan

Private Joseph Lawton Denton 29075
2nd Battalion Border Regiment

Joseph Lawton Denton was born in Holywell in 1879. On the 1881 census the Denton family resided at the Anchor Inn High Street Holywell. Head of the family was Henry Denton aged 43 and was the Inn Keeper, his Wife Jane Denton aged 37, Daughter Mary aged 13 and 3 Sons, John Henry aged 8, James Iorwerth aged 5 and Joseph Lawton aged 2. All the family were still at the Anchor Inn at the time of the 1891 census with an additional member of the family, Daughter Ethel aged 7.

The 1901 census shows Jane was now a widow aged 58 and had taken over the licence of the Anchor Inn following the death of her Husband Henry. Joseph still lived at the address and was a self-employed Butcher/Grocer. Ethel, now 17, was also at the public house.

The 1911 census shows Joseph living at 69 High Street, Bethesda where he was employed as a Butcher.

On 29th December 1912 aged 34, Joseph married Edna Lyons aged 30 years at Holywell Parish Church, Brynford Street Holywell.

Joseph was killed in action on Friday 26th October 1917 during the Third Battle of Ypres known as the Battle of Passendale. He is buried at Hooge Crater Cemetery, Plot VII, Row D, Grave 13.

- **To read more details on the Border Regiment Joseph Lawton Denton served with, the 2nd Battalion Border Regiment see Chapter 4 of this book**

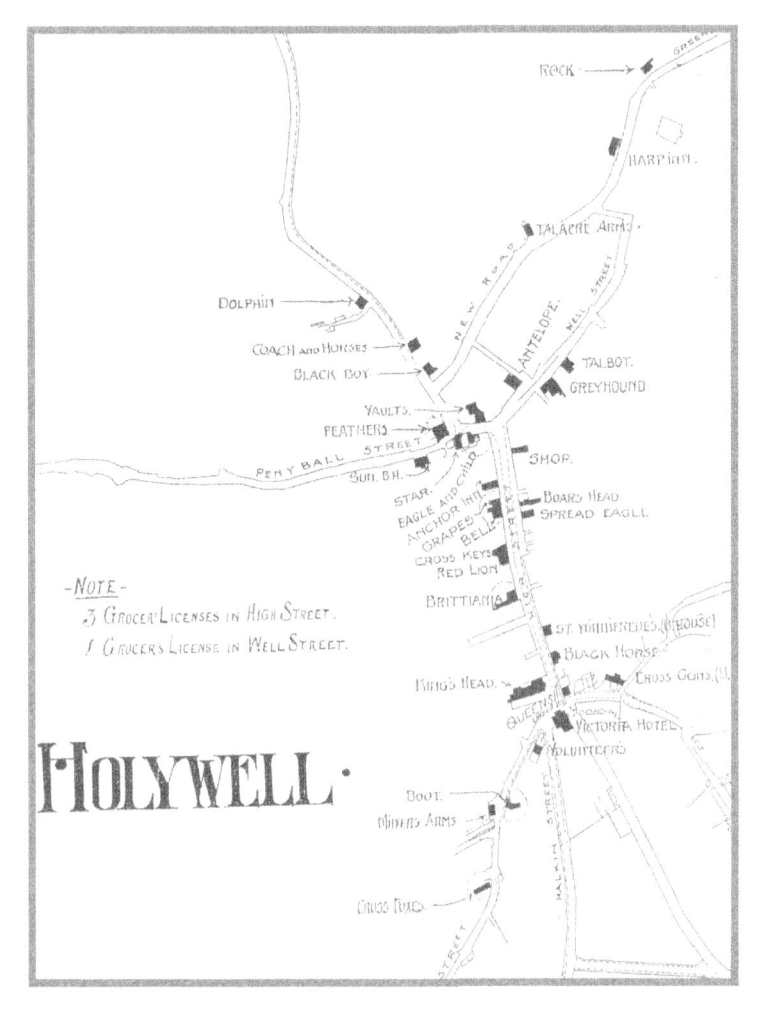

The Anchor Inn is shown on this 1904 map of Holywell

The Anchor Inn is situated on the High Street In-between the Eagle & Child and The Grapes

*Map kindly donated by Brian Taylor

Private 29075 Joseph Lawton Denton

Personal effects returned to his family

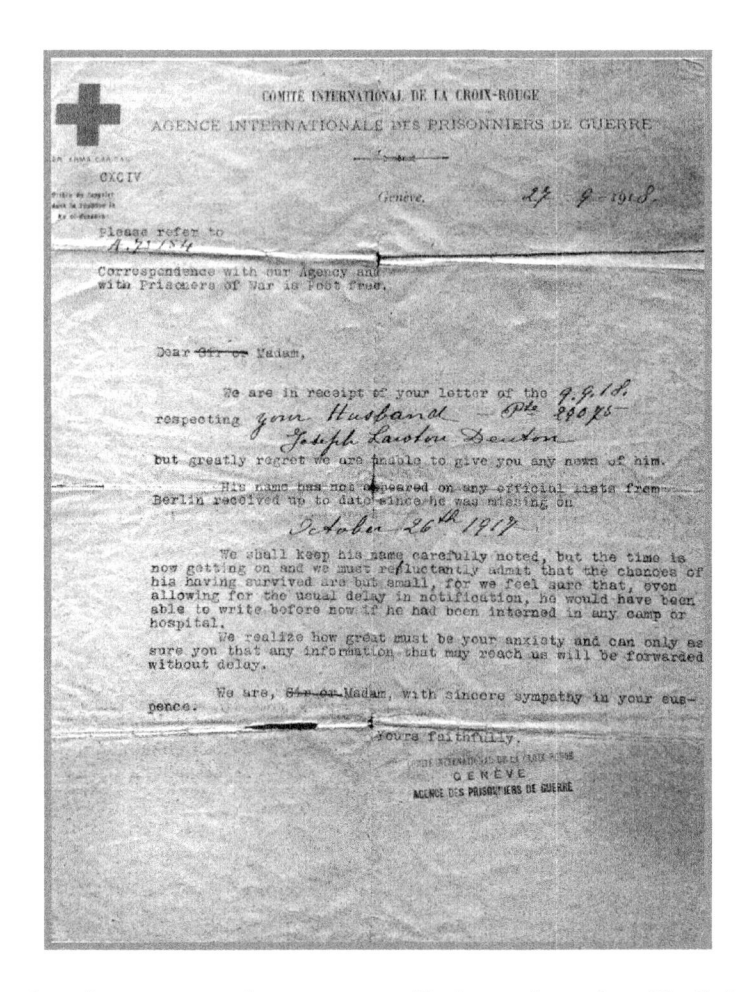

Joseph was missing for over a year. The letter above, from The Red Cross, made a gentle attempt to break the news to the family that he was almost certainly dead.

Information kindly provided by a family member Nick Denton

Plaque on St. James' Parish Church wall, Holywell

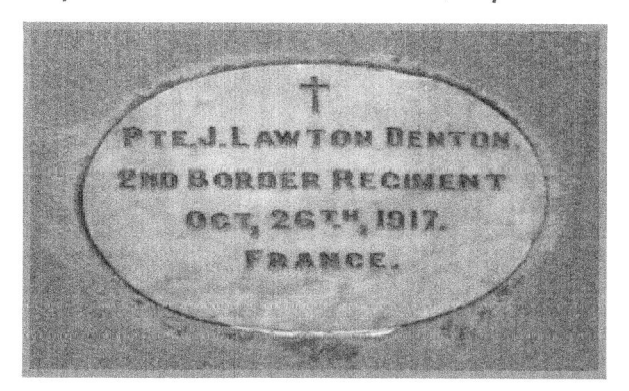

Pte. J. Lawton Denton,
2nd Border Regiment
Oct, 26th, 1917.
France.

Gravestone at Hooge Cemetery, Plot VII, Row D, Grave 13

Private Benjamin Edwards 20062
5th Battalion Royal Welsh Fusiliers

Benjamin Edwards was born in Holywell in 1870. The 1891 census shows that the family lived at Caernarfon Castle Hotel, Raven Court, Holywell. The Head of the family was John Edwards aged 57, who was employed as a Lead Miner, his Wife Sarah aged 56 was the Inn Keeper, their Son Benjamin aged 21 was also a Miner and Robert aged 8.

The 1901 census shows that Sarah who was now a widow aged 66 and was the Inn Keeper of the Abbotts Arms Hotel Pen-Y-Maes, Holywell. Benjamin aged 30 was now employed as a General Labourer and younger Brother Robert aged 18 was a Locomotive Stoker.

The 1911 census stated that the family were still living in the Abbotts Arms Hotel Pen-y-Maes.

Benjamin Edwards enlisted on the 12th of April 1915 at Queensferry. He joined the No. 1 Supply Company 5th Battalion Royal Welsh Fusiliers. He declared that he had previously served with, resigned from 2nd Battalion R. W. F., and gave his occupation as Barman.

He was discharged on 17.03.1916 after being examined in Chester on 03.03.1916. He was diagnosed with complicated aortic heart disease, which responded to treatment by digitalis (an extract from the foxglove plant), but to no real extent and the prognosis was "not good." He was permanently discharged from War Service, Home Service and Light Service. His illness was not caused by Military Service and there is no mention of him serving abroad. The form states that his home address at this time as 5 Abbotts Cottages, Pen-y-Maes. Holywell.

Benjamin died on 29th May 1916 and is buried at Greenfield Cemetery.

He is remembered on the North Wales Heroes' Memorial Arch in Bangor.

- To read more details on the Battalion that Benjamin Edward's served, the 5th Battalion Royal Welsh Fusiliers see Chapter 4 of this book

The Abbotts Arms Hotel, Pen-y-Maes, Holywell

Greenfield Cemetery where Benjamin Edwards is buried

Authors own photograph

Private Robert Edwards 241143
5th Battalion Royal Welsh Fusiliers

Robert Edwards was born in Holywell in 1882. The 1901 census shows the family lived at 6 Bagillt Street, Holywell. The Head of the family was Samuel Edwards a 40-year-old Head Smelter, his Wife Sarah Ann aged 39 and their 3 Children, Robert aged 19 who was employed as a Compositor at a local Printing Company, Elizabeth aged 17 a trainee School Teacher and Joseph aged 16 a Plasterer.

Robert married Mary Francis in 1907 at the English Presbyterian Chapel, Chester Road Flint.

The 1911 census tells us they have a 12month old Son Joseph Harold Edwards. Robert is still employed as a Compositor and the family live at 1 Garth-y-Foel, Holywell. Prior to Robert enlisting with the Royal Welsh Fusiliers in 1915 the family had moved to Ty Coch, Pen-y-Ball, Holywell.

Robert arrived in the Balkans with the Battalion on Sunday 8th August 1915.

Robert was killed in action on the first day of the Battle of Gaza on Monday 26th March 1917 aged 35 years.

He is also remembered on the North Wales Heroes' Memorial Arch in Bangor.

He is remembered on the Jerusalem Memorial Panel 20-22.

- **To read more details on the Battalion Robert Edwards served with, the 5th Battalion Royal Welsh Fusiliers see Chapter 4 of this book**

Private Robert Edwards 241143

Jerusalem Memorial – Panel 20-22

Second Lieutenant David Edward Evans
3rd Battalion Royal Welsh Fusiliers

David Edward Evans was born in 1891 and during his early years lived at Hendwr, Llandrillo, Merionethsire with his Father Robert Evans.

Sometime prior to 1911 he moved to Holywell where he was employed as a Grocer's Assistant.

The 1911 census states that he was living at that time with his Uncle William Hammond and family at Bryn Caesar, Holywell. People listed living here were Hugh William Hammond aged 55, Hugh Wyn Hammond, aged 23, Mary Hammond aged 21, David Edward Evans aged 20, Elizabeth Catherine Owen aged 26, Annie Keyiah Price aged 15, Arthur Price aged 33 and Edward John Jones aged 28.

He married Vera and they lived at Blodwen Villas, Holywell, she later moved to Hopefield, Holywell.

He was killed in action at the Battle of Albert, 26th August 1918 and buried at Caterpillar Valley Cemetery, Longueval, The Somme, aged 27. Plot VII Row B Grave 16.

He is also remembered on the North Wales Heroes' Memorial Arch in Bangor.

- **To read more details on the Battalion David Edward Evans served with, the 3rd Battalion Royal Welsh Fusiliers see Chapter 4 of this book**

Caterpillar Valley Cemetery Longueval Somme

Plot VII. Row B. Grave 16

DAVID E. EVANS.
2ND LIEUT 3RD. R.W.F.
AUG 26TH. 1918.
FRANCE.

Plaque on St. James' Parish Church wall, Holywell

Medal Card of David Edward Evans

These medal cards were created by the Army Medal Office towards the end of the First World War. They record the medals that men and women who served in the First World War were entitled to claim

Arthur Henry Fisher – Able Seaman 8191
Royal Navy 309518

Arthur Henry Fisher was born in Stroud Gloucestershire on 31st May 1883.

Very little is known of his early life.

Arthur married Lily Victoria Cordelia Baily in 1907 and they lived at 40 Cottage View, Arundel Street, Landport, Portsmouth.

They had 2 Children, Evelyn Nellie Cordialia Fisher and Arthur Henry Fisher. At some time prior to the First World War Arthur lived in Brynford Street, Holywell.

In the 1911 census Arthur was 29 and his occupation was Seaman with the Royal Navy.

Arthur drowned serving with The Royal Australian Navy on the 14th of September 1914 on his Majesty's Australian Submarine AE1 in St. George's Channel, New Britain, Papua New Guinea, aged 32.

Arthur is remembered on the North Wales Heroes' Memorial Arch in Bangor and Plymouth Navel Memorial, Panel 1 Commemorative Area.

Plaque on St. James' Parish Church wall, Holywell

Plymouth Navel Memorial, Panel 1 Commemorative Area

H.M.A.S. A.E.1 Submarine

- To read more details about Arthur Henry Fisher's story of his Submarine see Chapter 4 of this book

Company Quartermaster Sergeant Alfred Thomas Hinsley

Royal Defence Corps

Alfred Thomas Hinsley was born in Carlton Selby, Yorkshire in October 1869.

The 1881 census tells us that the family lived in Lower Street Carlton, Selby Yorkshire. The Head of the family was Thomas Hinsley aged 47, a Gardener's Labourer, Bridget Hinsley, his Wife, aged 45 and Alfred Thomas Hinsley aged 11. Thomas died aged 50 in 1884 and his Wife Bridget died in 1890 aged 54

The 1901 census shows that Alfred is now married to Frances Bacon Hinsley aged 33. Alfred was employed as a Foreman in a Joinery Shop and they resided at 75 Kilburn Lane, Willesdon London and have 3 Children, Edna Mary Hinsley aged 6, Beatrice Annie Hinsley aged 5 and Ernest Thomas Hinsley aged 2. By 1911 census the family have moved to 1 Callcot Road Brandesbury, London. Alfred was employed as a Clerk of Works and now has a further 3 Children, Madeline age 9, Muriel Frances aged 7 and Agnes aged 0.

Alfred enlisted with the Royal Welsh Fusiliers at the Drill Hall, Halkyn Street, Holywell before being transferred to the Royal Defence Corps.

He died of self-inflicted wounds while in a state of temporary insanity due to a disease contracted on active service, 21st May 1917 aged 47. His widow and children's address is given as 88 Wickham Road, Brockley, SE London. There is no record of the family living in Holywell, but we do know that Alfred is buried in Holywell Cemetery, Fron Park Road, Holywell.

He is also remembered on the North Wales Heroes' Memorial Arch in Bangor.

- To read more details about the Battalion Alfred Thomas Hinsley served with, the Royal Defence Corps. see Chapter 4 of this book

Alfred Thomas Hinsley's Gravestone at Holywell Cemetery, Fron Park Road

Author's own photograph

Last known address of where Alfred Thomas Hinsley lived

Private Edward Samuel Hughes 203257
16th Battalion Royal Welsh Fusiliers

Edward Samuel Hughes was born in Holywell in 1894.

The 1911 census states that the family lived at the Harp Inn, Greenfield Road, Holywell. The Head of the family was Thomas Hughes aged 60 who was the Inn Keeper, his Wife Elizabeth Ann aged 56 and their 3 Children, Mary Catherine aged 32, Edward Samuel aged 17 who was employed as a Piercer in the Weaving Factory and Aaron aged 18 who was also a Piercer, both boys were employed by the Welsh Flannel Mill.

Edward married Elizabeth Reece on 22 April 1915 and lived at 1 Crescent Bank, Greenfield.

On 11th December 1915 aged 22, Edward enlisted as a Private with the 4th Battalion Royal Welsh Fusiliers, later transferring to the 16th Battalion Royal Welsh Fusiliers.

He embarked for France on 2nd August 1917 and was killed in action just over a month later on the 19th of September 1917 during the Third Battle of Ypres.

Edward is also remembered on the North Wales Heroes' memorial Arch in Bangor.

He is buried at Erqinghem-Lys Churchyard Extension, Plot II, Row F, Grave 10.

- To read more details on the Battalion where Edward Samuel Hughes served, the 16th Battalion Royal Welsh Fusiliers - see Chapter 4 of this book

HOLYWELL.

PTE EDWARD SAMUEL HUGHES, Aged 23 years, killed in action. Son of the late Mr Thos Hughes, Harp Inn, and of Mrs Hughes, Greenfield Terrace. Prior to joining the Army he was employed at the Textile Mills.

An article in the County Herald 12th October 1917

The Welsh Flannel Mill, Holywell, where Edward and his Brother Aaron worked

Erqinghem-Lys Churchyard Extension – Plot 11. Row F, Grave 10

Where Edward is buried

Address where Edward lived when married in 1915 – Crescent Bank, Greenfield, Holywell

The Harp Inn, (centre of picture), Greenfield Road, Holywell where Private Edward Samuel Hughes lived with his family on the 1911 census

Private William Hughes 26435
17th Battalion Welsh Fusiliers

William Hughes was born in Holywell in 1898.

The 1901 census shows the family lived at Pwlleiai, Brynford, Holywell. Head of the family was John Hughes aged 35, employed as a Coal Miner, his Wife Mary aged 31 and their 4 Children, Edward aged 10, Edwin aged 6, William aged 3 and Henry aged 1 month.

The 1911 census shows that the family lived at 3 Primrose Hill, Holywell. John was 46 and still a Coal Miner, Mary his first Wife had died, and John was now married to Jane who was 28. They had 3 Children, Gladys aged 6, Sarah aged 4 and Benjamin aged 2. Also living with them were the 4 Children from John's previous marriage, Edward aged 20, a Coal Miner, Edwin aged 16, William aged 13 and Henry aged 11.

William served with the 14th Battalion Royal Welsh Fusiliers and arrived in France on 4th December 1915. He was killed in action on 20th May 1916 aged 18 years.

William is remembered on the North Wales Heroes' Memorial Arch in Bangor.

The personal inscription on Williams Grave in France, Merville Communal Cemetery, Plot VI, Row P, Grave 5, reads: -

"In life we loved you, in death sweet memories cling"

- To read more details on the Battalion William Hughes served with, the 17th Battalion Royal Welsh Fusiliers see Chapter 4 of this book

Merville Communal Cemetery

IN LIFE
WE LOVED YOU DEARLY
IN DEATH
SWEET MEMORIES CLING

Plot VI, Row P, Grave 5

The next of kin for William Hughes would have been sent this Death Plaque after the War to commemorate all of the War dead. Over 1 million were issued in total.

Second Lieutenant Percy William Jervis
3/5th Battalion Royal Welsh Fusiliers

Percy William Jervis was born on 23rd April 1885 and christened on 31st May 1885

The 1891 England census shows the family living at Spring Blower, Shifnal.

The Head of the family William Jervis was a 39-year-old widower and was a self-employed Baker and Grocer. He has 2 Children, Mabel Jervis aged 11 and Percy William Jervis aged 5. Also living in the house was William's Mother Sarah, aged 71 and his Sister Amelia aged 27. In the 1911 census Percy was still living at home in Shifnal, Shropshire, aged 25. William, his Father was 57, Amelia Elizabeth Jervis (Williams Sister) was 47, Norman Alfred Jervis, the Brother of Percy, aged 17 and Millicent Mary Jarvis, Percy's Sister, aged 12.

Percy enlisted in the 3/5th Battalion Royal Welsh Fusiliers on the 20th of November 1915. His profession at the time of enlistment was Account Clerk to the Holywell Brand of Guardians & Rural District Council. The address given for any correspondence was "Tros-y-Maes, Holywell." Percy previously served with the 1st Shropshire Light Infantry Volunteer Force as a Private until 1907.

Percy was later attached to the 1st Battalion Royal Welsh Fusiliers and served as Second Lieutenant. He was killed in action at Bapume, Somme, France on Tuesday 3rd April 1917 aged 31.

His next of kin was his Father William, as Percy never married. He is buried at St. Ledger British Cemetery in Pas De Calais, Grave A2.

He is also remembered on the North Wales Heroes' Memorial Arch in Bangor.

- To read more details on the Battalion Percy William Jarvis served with, the 3/5th Battalion Royal Welsh Fusiliers see Chapter 4 of this book

St. Ledger British Cemetery, Pas De Calis, Grave A2

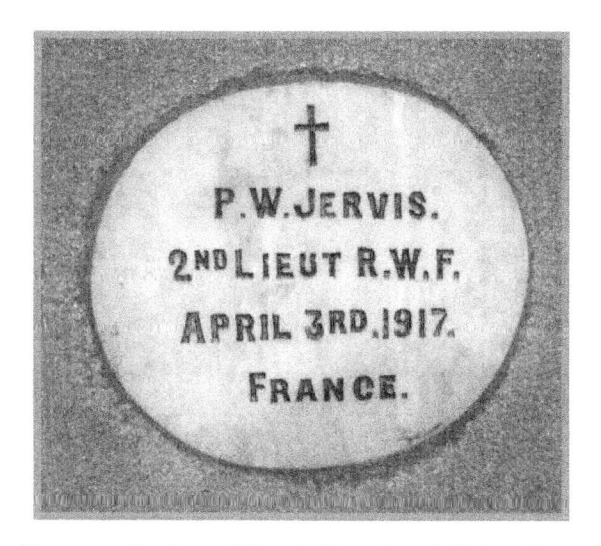

Plaque on St. James' Parish Church wall, Holywell

Army Form E. 536.

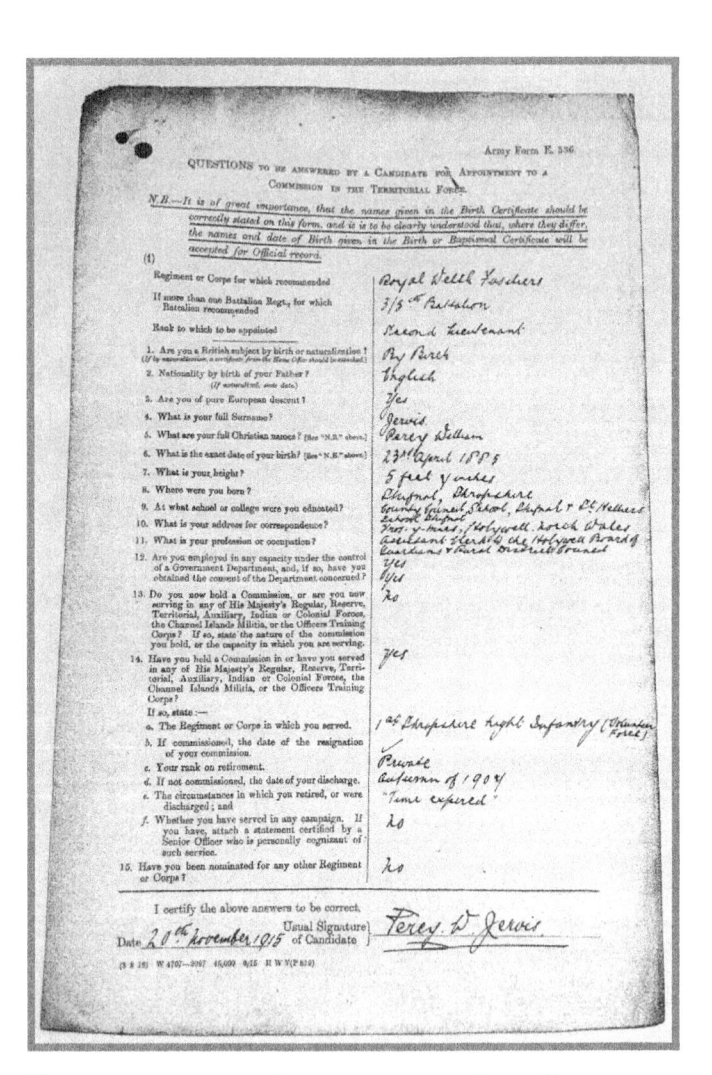

QUESTIONS TO BE ANSWERED BY A CANDIDATE FOR APPOINTMENT TO A COMMISSION IN THE TERRITORIAL FORCE.

N.B.—It is of great importance, that the names given in the Birth Certificate should be correctly stated on this form, and it is to be clearly understood that, where they differ, the names and date of Birth given in the Birth or Baptismal Certificate will be accepted for Official record.

(1)

Regiment or Corps for which recommended	Royal Welsh Fusiliers
If more than one Battalion Regt., for which Battalion recommended	3/5th Battalion
Rank to which to be appointed	Second Lieutenant
1. Are you a British subject by birth or naturalization? (If by naturalization, a certificate from the Home Office should be attached.)	By Birth
2. Nationality by birth of your Father? (If naturalized, state date.)	English
3. Are you of pure European descent?	Yes
4. What is your full Surname?	Jervis
5. What are your full Christian names? (See "N.B." above.)	Percy William
6. What is the exact date of your birth? (See "N.B." above.)	23rd April 1889
7. What is your height?	5 feet 9 inches
8. Where were you born?	Shifnal, Shropshire
9. At what school or college were you educated?	County Council School, Shifnal & St Hellens School, Shifnal
10. What is your address for correspondence?	Tros-y-mias, Holywell, North Wales
11. What is your profession or occupation?	Assistant Clerk to the Holywell Board of Guardians & Rural District Council
12. Are you employed in any capacity under the control of a Government Department, and, if so, have you obtained the consent of the Department concerned?	Yes Yes
13. Do you now hold a Commission, or are you now serving in any of His Majesty's Regular, Reserve, Territorial, Auxiliary, Indian or Colonial Forces, the Channel Islands Militia, or the Officers Training Corps? If so, state the nature of the commission you hold, or the capacity in which you are serving.	No
14. Have you held a Commission in or have you served in any of His Majesty's Regular, Reserve, Territorial, Auxiliary, Indian or Colonial Forces, the Channel Islands Militia, or the Officers Training Corps?	Yes
If so, state:—	
a. The Regiment or Corps in which you served.	1st Shropshire Light Infantry (Volunteer Force)
b. If commissioned, the date of the resignation of your commission.	
c. Your rank on retirement.	Private
d. If not commissioned, the date of your discharge.	Autumn of 1907
e. The circumstances in which you retired, or were discharged; and	"Time expired"
f. Whether you have served in any campaign. If you have, attach a statement certified by a Senior Officer who is personally cognizant of such service.	No
15. Have you been nominated for any other Regiment or Corps?	No

I certify the above answers to be correct.

Date 20th November 1915   Usual Signature of Candidate   Percy W. Jervis

This is a questionnaire, for commission to Second Lieutenant

REPORT OF THE STANDING COMMITTEE OF ADJUSTMENT.

(AFFAIRS OF DECEASED OFFICERS.)

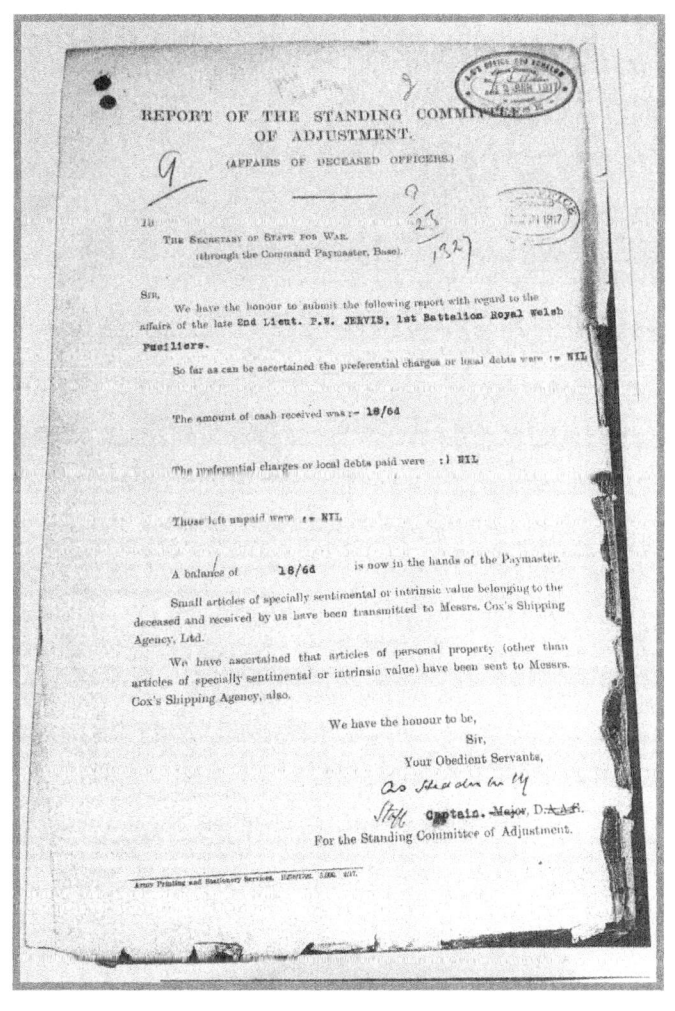

To
THE SECRETARY OF STATE FOR WAR.
(through the Command Paymaster, Base).

Sir,

We have the honour to submit the following report with regard to the affairs of the late 2nd Lieut. P.W. JERVIS, 1st Battalion Royal Welsh Fusiliers.

So far as can be ascertained the preferential charges or local debts were :- NIL

The amount of cash received was :- 18/6d

The preferential charges or local debts paid were :) NIL

Those left unpaid were :- NIL

A balance of 18/6d is now in the hands of the Paymaster.

Small articles of specially sentimental or intrinsic value belonging to the deceased and received by us have been transmitted to Messrs. Cox's Shipping Agency, Ltd.

We have ascertained that articles of personal property (other than articles of specially sentimental or intrinsic value) have been sent to Messrs. Cox's Shipping Agency, also.

We have the honour to be,
Sir,
Your Obedient Servants,

Captain, Major, D.A.A.G.
For the Standing Committee of Adjustment.

This is a document, "Affairs of the Deceased Officer" for Percy William Jervis

Roll of Honour - The Men on the Holywell Memorial

Part 2

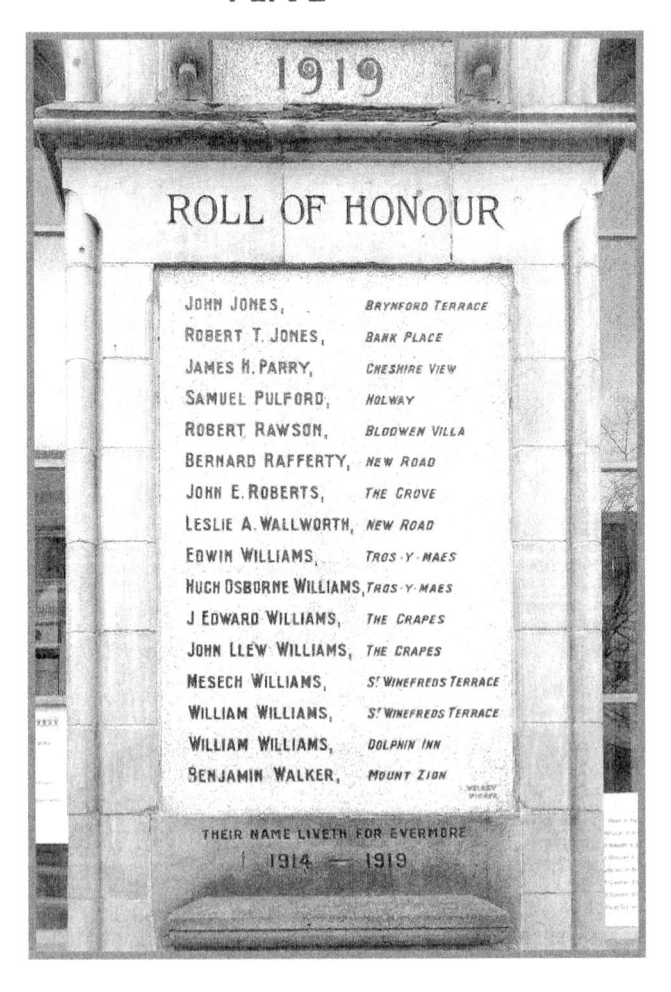

ROLL OF HONOUR

JOHN JONES,	BRYNFORD TERRACE
ROBERT T. JONES,	BANK PLACE
JAMES H. PARRY,	CHESHIRE VIEW
SAMUEL PULFORD,	HOLWAY
ROBERT RAWSON,	BLODWEN VILLA
BERNARD RAFFERTY,	NEW ROAD
JOHN E. ROBERTS,	THE GROVE
LESLIE A. WALLWORTH,	NEW ROAD
EDWIN WILLIAMS,	TROS-Y-MAES
HUGH OSBORNE WILLIAMS,	TROS-Y-MAES
J EDWARD WILLIAMS,	THE CRAPES
JOHN LLEW WILLIAMS,	THE CRAPES
MESECH WILLIAMS,	ST WINEFREDS TERRACE
WILLIAM WILLIAMS,	ST WINEFREDS TERRACE
WILLIAM WILLIAMS,	DOLPHIN INN
BENJAMIN WALKER,	MOUNT ZION

THEIR NAME LIVETH FOR EVERMORE
1914 — 1919

Private John Jones 20903
The King's Liverpool Regiment

John Jones was born in Greenfield, near Holywell, Flintshire in 1862.

The 1881 census states that the family lived in Spring Bank, Greenfield. Head of the family Isaac Jones aged 48, a Farmer's Labourer, his Wife Sarah Jones aged 42 and 4 Sons, John aged 19, who was employed as a Brewer's Carter (drove a horse-drawn cart containing beer barrels), Isaac aged 17, a Domestic Servant, Owen Jones aged 13 and Robert Jones aged 10.

John married Mary and they lived at 33 Lucania Street, Garston, Liverpool.

John was serving with the 8th Supernumerary C.O.Y. 3/5th Battalion of the King's Liverpool Regiment.

John died on Thursday 15th June 1916 aged 53 and is buried in Allerton Cemetery, Liverpool. Grave IV Gen. Div. 666.

- To read more details on the Regiment that John Jones served with, the Kings Liverpool Regiment see Chapter 4 of this book

Allerton Cemetery Liverpool

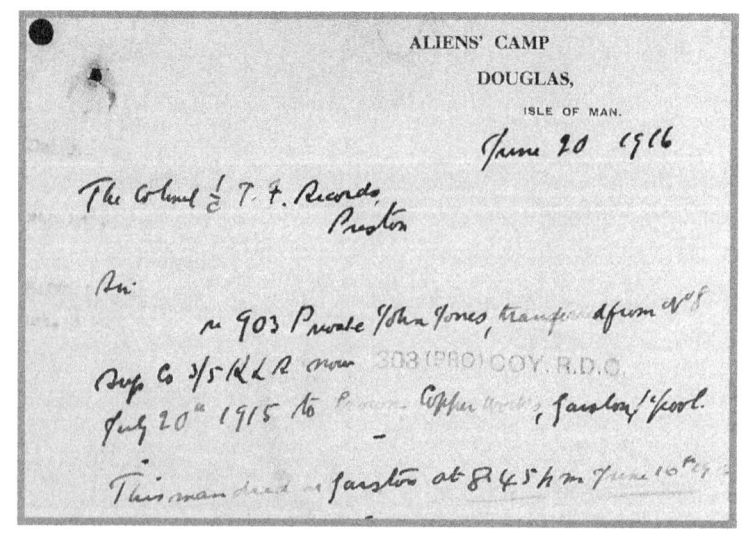

Document sent to Record Office, to updated them of the death of John Jones

Document showing cause of death of John Jones

Typical horse drawn cart used by John Jones

Corporal Robert Thomas Jones 505068
1st/13th (County of London) Battalion (Princess Louise's Kensington Battalion)

Nothing is known about the early life of Robert Thomas Jones. He married Elizabeth Ann Davies on 4th August 1917 aged 28, Elizabeth was 31, at Holywell Parish Church. They lived at 7 Brognallt, Holywell Flintshire.

Robert's Father was William Edward Jones, who was employed as a Painter.

Robert was killed in action on Thursday 11th April 1918. He is buried at Calais Dainville Communal Cemetery, Pas De Calais. B8.

The personal inscription on his headstone was

"He gave up wife, home and country for others"

He is also remembered on the North Wales Heroes' Memorial Arch in Bangor.

- To read more details on the Battalion Robert Thomas Jones served with, the 1st/13th Battalion see Chapter 4 of this book

ROBERT THOMAS JONES
SEC! B.C. 1|13. LONDON REG
FRANCE APRIL 12TH 1918.

Plaque on St. James' Parish Church wall, Holywell

Dainville Communal Cemetery, Pas De Calais. Grave B8

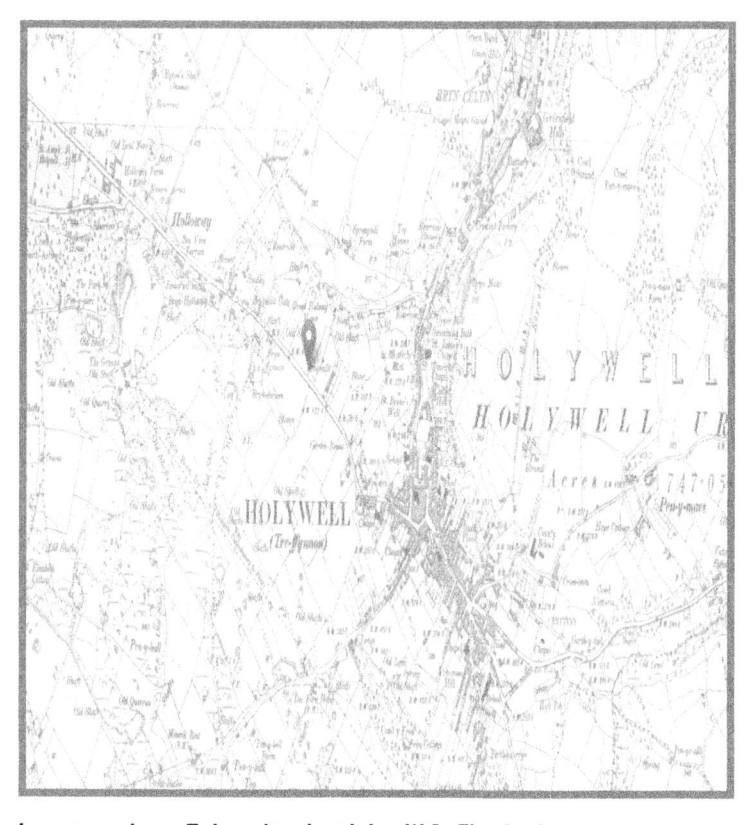

Location where Robert lived with his Wife Elizabeth –

7 Brognallt, Holywell, Flintshire

*https://historicplacenames.rcahmw.gov.uk

Gunner James Henry Parry 156286
78th Siege Battery, Royal Garrison Artillery

James Henry Parry was born in Holywell, Flintshire in 1888.

The 1911 census states the family lived at 1 Red House, Holywell, Flintshire. The Head of the family was James Parry, a widower, who was 56. He was employed as a Woollen Carder in the Welsh Flannel Mill, Greenfield Road, Holywell. He had 6 Children, Joseph Edward Parry, 26 a Lead Smelter, James Henry Parry, aged 23, a Woollen Card Cleaner, Margaret Jane Parry, aged 20, a Flannel Weaver, Caroline Parry, aged 17, also a Flannel Weaver, Mary Ellen aged 28 and Muriel Parry aged 14.

James Henry Parry married Gwladys Mary Parry on 22nd April 1912, and they lived at New Houses, Strand, Holywell.

James was killed in action on Sunday 30th June 1918 aged 29 and is buried at Wailly Orchard Cemetery, Pas De Calais, Plot III, Row G, Grave 2.

He is also remembered on the North Wales Heroes' Memorial Arch in Bangor.

- **To read more details on James Henry Parry's 78th Siege Battery, Royal Garrison Artillery see Chapter 4 of this book**

Wailly Orchard Cemetery, Pas De Calais,

Plot III, Row G, Grave 2

Plaque on St. James' Parish Church wall, Holywell

This is the type of machine that James Henry Parry would have worked on

Carding: the fibres are separated and then assembled into a loose strand (sliver or tow) at the conclusion of this stage.

> The cotton comes off of the picking machine in laps, and is then taken to carding machines. The carders line up the fibres nicely to make them easier to spin. The carding machine consists mainly of one big roller with smaller ones surrounding it. All of the rollers are covered with small teeth, and as the cotton progresses further on the teeth get finer (i.e. closer together). The cotton leaves the carding machine in the form of a sliver; a large rope of fibres.[11]

The Seige Batteries of the Royal Garrison Artillery

Lieutenant Samuel Pulford
Royal Navy Reserve H. M. Tug "Stolic"

Samuel Pulford was born in Ysceifiog, Flintshire in 1862.

The 1871 census shows that the family lived in Holywell. The Head of the family was Peter Pulford, aged 53, who was a Tailor/Draper and a Grocer, his Wife, Elizabeth aged 52 and their 6 Children, Ann aged 30, a Grocer's Assistant, Jane aged 23, a Milliner, Elizabeth aged 21, Mary aged 15, Edward aged 11 and Samuel aged 8.

Samuel enlisted in the Merchant Navy on 19th November 1885 at the age of 23. He was awarded his Certificate of Compentency as a First Mate by the order of the Board of Trade. He eventually became a Master Mariner. On the 31st May 1890, he was First Mate on the Vessel SS Gorgon which sailed from Liverpool. He served on this ship until 9th August 1890.

Samuel married Elizabeth Jane Owen in 1907.

On 15th January 1915, he enlisted as a soldier in the Royal Welsh Horse Reserve, giving his age as 50, although he was actually 53. His short service certificate states that he was in service for the duration of the War, however, 5 months later on 11th July 1915 he was discharged as medically unfit.

The family, at this time, lived at Bodhyfryd Road, Holywell.

On the 19th November 1915, Samuel made an application to join the Baskingwerk Masonic Lodge, Colshill Street, Holywell and was inducted into the lodge on 25th August 1916.

Samuel returned to Plymouth and served as a Lieutenant on H. M. Tug Stolic. He died at the Royal Naval Reserve Hospital, Plymouth, on 26th June 1917 aged 55.

Following his death he received a Masonic Funeral at 2.30pm on Friday 29th June 1917 with the members of the Basingwerk Masonic Lodge wearing their Masonic regalia. They escorted the coffin to the Zion Cemetery in Carmel, Holywell, the place of internment. At the conclusion of the burial ceremony, all the members of the lodge dropped sprigs of Arcadia onto the coffin.

Samuel is also remembered on the Prestatyn and Mostyn War Memorials and the North Wales Heroes' Memorial Arch in Bangor.

- **To read more details on where Samuel Pulford served, the Royal Navy Reserve, H. M. Stolic see Chapter 4 of this book**

Samuel Pulford's Grave at Zion Cemetery, Carmel

*Authors own photographs

The Mostyn Memorial forms part of the pulpit in Christ Church, Mostyn

Prestatyn Memorial

H. M. Tug Stolic

Lance Corporal Robert Rawson 26534
12th Battalion Highland Light Infantry
(City of Glasgow Regiment)

Robert Rawson was born on 12th September 1886 at Dumfries Scotland.

The family moved from Scotland to South Wales in July 1889, when Robert was 3 years old. The family lived at 26 Crescent Street, Llanwchainarn, Montgomeryshire.

The 1911 census shows that the Rawson family had moved again to Cambrain Cottage, Newtown, Montgomeryshire. The Head of the family was John Rawson, aged 49, who was employed as Woollen Manufacturer Manager, his Wife Anne, aged 51 and 6 Children, Robert aged 25 who was a Woollen Designer, William aged 24, a Carding Engineer, John aged 22, a Draper's Assistant, Benjamin aged 14, Annie aged 17 a Millinery Apprentice and Gwendoline aged 11.

Robert married Annie Elsie (surname unknown) of Golden Newton in 1912. They lived at Blodwen Villa, Holywell. They possibly moved to Holywell to work in the Woollen Mill, but this is not confirmed.

Robert enlisted in Jedburgh, Roxburghshire. Robert was killed in action on Sunday 13th August 1916 aged 31 years, during the capture of Martinpuich, near Arras Pas De Calais. He was on the War Office casualty list as "missing" on the 20th of September 1916 and his body was never found. Robert is remembered on the Thiepval Memorial to the missing on the Somme.

He is also remembered on the North Wales Heroes' Memorial Arch in Bangor.

- To read more details on where Robert Rawson served, 12th Battalion Highland Light Infantry (City of Glasgow Regiment) see Chapter 4 of this book

Pier and Face 15C at the Thiepval Memorial, France, showing the name of Lance Corporal Robert Rawson

Thiepval Memorial France

Authors own photograph

Robert Rawson's Medal Index card

Private John Bernard Rafferty 290485
Pembroke Yeomanry

John Bernard Rafferty was born in Holywell in 1900.

The 1901 census states that the family lived at 9 Bluebell Yard, Holywell.

Head of the family was Bernard Rafferty aged 34, who was employed as a Tinsmith, his Wife Mary Rafferty aged 26, who worked as a Hawker Tin Plate, Daughter's Mary aged 10, Edith aged 7, Margaret aged 5, Annie aged 3, Ellen aged 2 and their Son John Bernard aged 6 months.

John Joined the 5th Battalion Royal Welsh Fusiliers as a Boy Soldier. Then transferred to the Pembroke Yeomanry. He died on 8th November 1918 of influenza aged 18 and is buried in Holywell Cemetery. John is also remembered on the North Wales Heroes' Memorial Arch in Bangor.

- To read more details on John Bernard Rafferty's Pembroke Yeomanry see Chapter 4 of this book

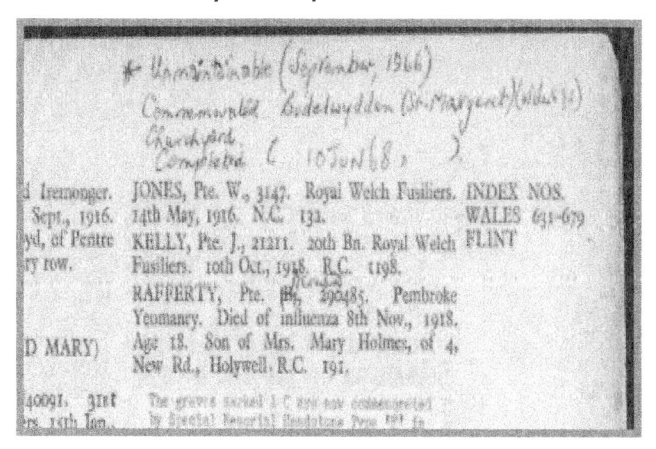

Commonwealth War Graves Commission Grave Details

Photograph of John Bernard Rafferty as a Boy Soldier. Service No. 2658

(Although we cannot identify John Bernard Rafferty above, the photograph was provided by a relative)

John Bernard Rafferty Pension Record

John Bernard Rafferty's Welsh Slate Headstone at Holywell Cemetery

Authors own photograph

Corporal John Edward Roberts 23754
10th Battalion Royal Welsh Fusiliers

John Edward Roberts was born in Holywell in 1893.
The 1911 census states that the family lived at 3 The Grove, Holywell. The Head of the family was John Roberts aged 41, a School Attendance Officer, his Wife Susannah aged 42, a Housewife and their 3 Children, John Edward Roberts aged 18 who was employed as a Auctioneers Clerk, Caradog Roberts aged 13 and Haydn Roberts aged 3.

John Edward Roberts enlisted as a Private with the Royal Welsh Fusiliers at Wrexham, aged 21 years and 10 months. Within a month of enlistment he was promoted to Lance Corporal on the 6th October 1914 and six days later was promoted again, to Corporal serving with the 10th Battalion in Belgium and France. John arrived in France on 28th September 1915 and was killed in action on 17th February 1916 aged 23 at Ypres. The local paper, The County Herald, printed extracts from letters from the family received from the Battalion Chaplin on Friday 8th March 1916.

"Corporal J. E. Roberts of the 10th Battalion, Royal Welsh Fusiliers, Son of Mr John Roberts, The Grove, Holywell has been killed by shell fire somewhere in France"

The sad news was conveyed in a letter from the Reverand David Cynddelw Williams, who was the Chaplin attached to the Battalion. The letter was received by the Father of the unfortunate young man last Friday morning in which the writer says -

"I am not sure whether you yet may have been informed that your dear Son, Corporal J. E. Roberts was taken away on Thursday morning last, I understand it was through shell fire and he could not have been concious of any pain, I cannot express my deepest sympathy with you as a family, in losing a happy and promising Son. I, as Chaplain, came frequently into contact with him and I came to understand him very well, frequently did I hear your Son sing "Lead Kindly Light" when at Bournmouth and I should say the the light did not fail him. Your Son was buried not far from the firing line".

John's grave was later lost due to shelling in the area.

He is remembered on the Menin Gate Memorial, Panel 22 in Ypres.

He is also remembered on the North Wales Heroes' Memorial Arch in Bangor.

- To read more details on John Edward Roberts 10th Battalion Royal Welsh Fusiliers see Chapter 4 of this book

Menin Gate Panel 22 where John Edward Roberts is Remembered

The Letter of the Attestation of Corporal J. E. Roberts 23754.

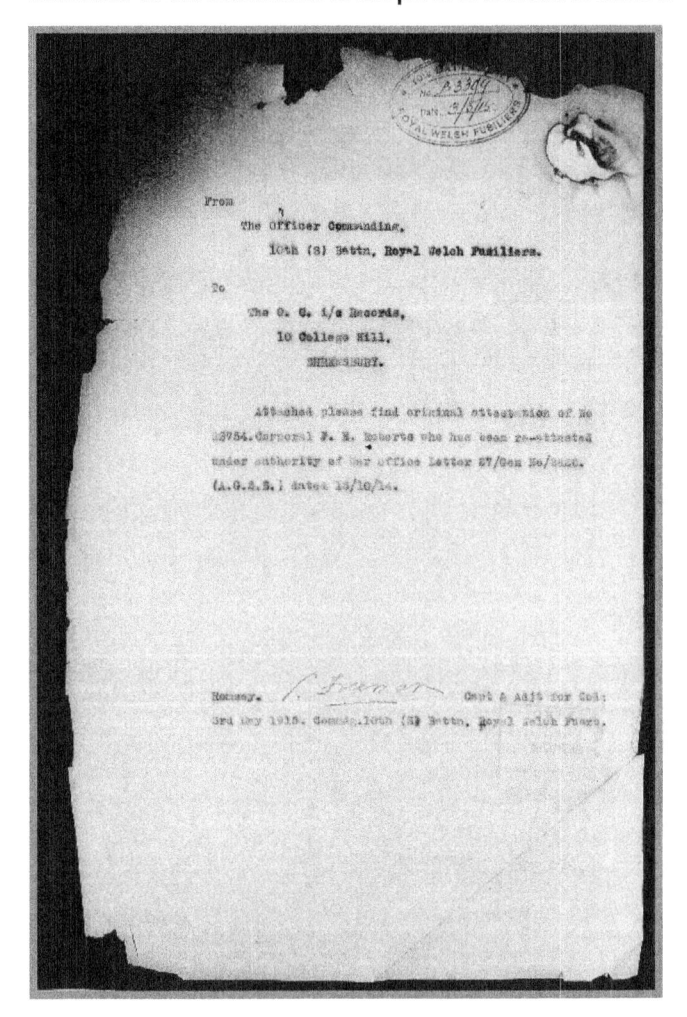

From

    The Officer Commanding,

        10th (S) Battn, Royal Welch Fusiliers.

To

    The O. C. i/c Records,

        10 College Hill,

        SHREWSBURY.

    Attached please find original attestation of No 23754. Corporal J. E. Roberts who has been re-attested under authority of War Office Letter 27/Gen No/2420. (A.G.4.B.) dated 15/10/14.

Romsey.   *(signature)*   Capt & Adjt for Col:
3rd May 1915.   Comdg.10th (S) Battn, Royal Welch Fusrs.

SHORT SERVICE.
(For the Duration of the War).

ATTESTATION OF

Name **John Edward Roberts** Corps **Royal Welsh Fus.**

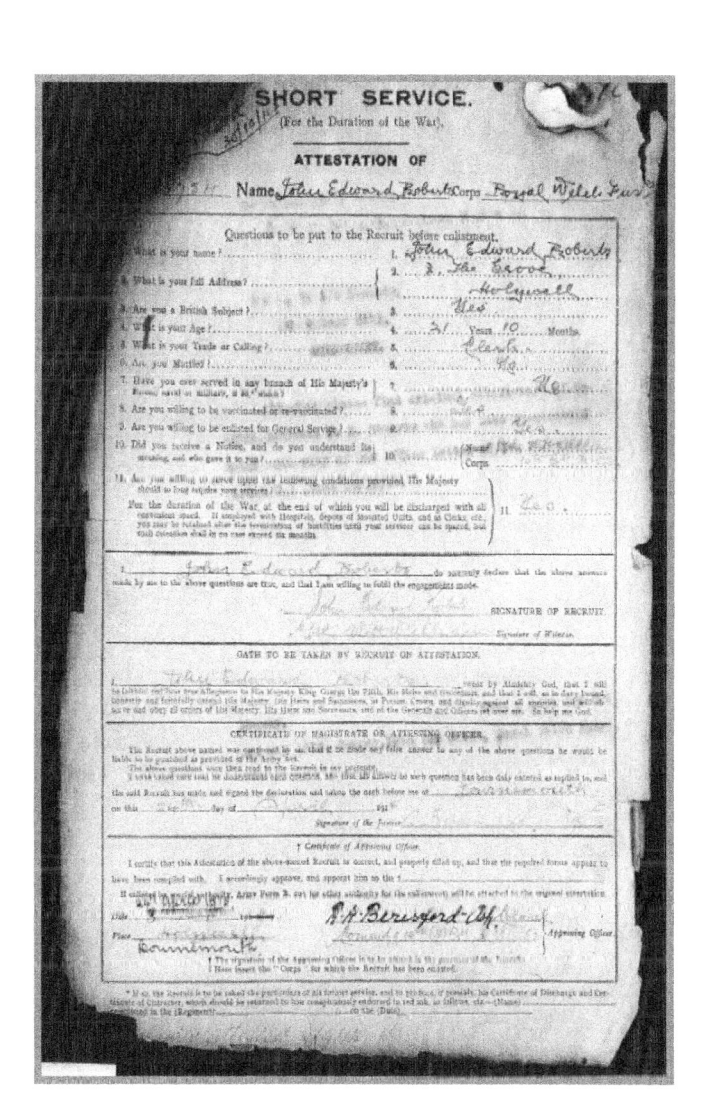

Questions to be put to the Recruit before enlistment.

1. What is your Name? — John Edward Roberts
2. What is your full Address? — 2, The Cross, Holywell
3. Are you a British Subject? — Yes
4. What is your Age? — 31 Years 10 Months
5. What is your Trade or Calling? — Clerk
6. Are you Married? — No
7. Have you ever served in any branch of His Majesty's Forces, naval or military, if so, which? — No
8. Are you willing to be vaccinated or re-vaccinated? —
9. Are you willing to be enlisted for General Service? —
10. Did you receive a Notice, and do you understand its meaning, and who gave it to you? —
11. Are you willing to serve upon the following conditions provided His Majesty should so long require your services? — Yes

For the duration of the War, at the end of which you will be discharged with all convenient speed. If employed with Hospitals, Depots of Mounted Units, and as Clerks, etc., you may be retained after the termination of hostilities until your services can be spared, but such retention shall in no case exceed six months.

I, John Edward Roberts, do solemnly declare that the above answers made by me to the above questions are true, and that I am willing to fulfil the engagements made.

SIGNATURE OF RECRUIT
Signature of Witness

OATH TO BE TAKEN BY RECRUIT ON ATTESTATION.

I, John Edward Roberts, swear by Almighty God, that I will be faithful and bear true Allegiance to His Majesty King George the Fifth, His Heirs and Successors, and that I will, as in duty bound, honestly and faithfully defend His Majesty, His Heirs and Successors, in Person, Crown, and Dignity against all enemies, and will observe and obey all orders of His Majesty, His Heirs and Successors, and of the Generals and Officers set over me. So help me God.

CERTIFICATE OF MAGISTRATE OR ATTESTING OFFICER.

The Recruit above named was cautioned by me that if he made any false answer to any of the above questions he would be liable to be punished as provided in the Army Act.
The above questions were then read to the Recruit in my presence.
I have taken care that he understands each question, and that his answer to each question has been duly entered as replied to, and the said Recruit has made and signed the declaration and taken the oath before me at _____
on this _____ day of _____ 19__

Signature of the Justice

† Certificate of Approving Officer

I certify that this Attestation of the above-named Recruit is correct, and properly filled up, and that the required forms appear to have been complied with. I accordingly approve, and appoint him to the ‡

P. A. Beresford

Place **Bournemouth**

† The signature of the Approving Officer is to be in that in which the particulars of the Recruit.
‡ Here insert the " Corps " for which the Recruit has been enlisted.

Held at the National Archives

Sergeant Leslie Alfred Wallworth
5th Battalion Royal Welsh Fusiliers

Leslie Alfred Wallworth was born on 21st November 1892 at 23 Rendal Street, Everton, West Derby, Liverpool.

The 1891 census, a year before Leslie's birth, states that the family lived at 263 Brook Street, Everton, West Derby, Liverpool.

The Head of the family was Harold Wallworth aged 26, who was employed as The Richmond Hotel, Liverpool as a Manager, his Wife Mary Wallworth aged 22 and their 10 month old Daughter Florence Wallworth.

By the 1901 census the family had relocated to North Wales. They lived at 4 Cross Street, Holywell, Flintshire. Harold was employed in a local public house as a Barman. Mary his Wife, was also employed at the same public house as a Domestic Housekeeper. Sadly, it is believed that Florance, their Daughter had died by this time. The other 2 Children listed on the census were Leslie now aged 8 and his Sister Maud aged 6.

On the 1911 census Leslie aged 18 is recorded as being an inmate at Bradwell Reformatory School for Boys. Boys were admitted to Bradwell from the North of the Country. The boys learned how to farm and upon release, many were placed in apprenticeships with local farmers. It is not known exactly why Leslie ended up there.

The 1911 census shows that the family now live at the Old Gate House, Holywell. Harold is now 46 and is employed as a Singer Sewing Machinist.

Leslie, on returning to the family home, then enlisted as a Soldier in the 5th Battalion Royal Welsh Fusiliers at the Drill Hall in Halkyn Street in 1914, rising to the rank of Sergeant.

Leslie arrived with the 5th Battalion at Gallipoli on the 8th of August 1915 and was killed in action two days later on the 10th August aged 22 years. His body was never found and Leslie is remembered on The Helles Memorial, Gallipoli. Panels 77 to 80.

- To find out more about Leslie Alfred Wallworth's 5th Battalion Royal Welsh Fusiliers see chapter 4 of this book

This is Bradwell Reformatory School for Boys, where Leslie Alfred Wallworth was sent to. The school was founded by George William Latham in 1855, following an 1854 Act of Parliament. This ruled that children under the age of 16, convicted of a criminal offence, could be sent to Reformatory School, a penal and educational institution for children

Leslie Alfred Wallworth

Plaque on St. James' Parish Church wall, Holywell

Helles Memorial, Gallipoli

Sergt. Leslie Wallworth.

It is with regret and sympathy for his widowed mother that the news from a number of sources was received that Sergeant Leslie Wallworth, of Holywell, had lost his life in the gallant fight of the 1/5th Battalion R.W.F. at their landing on the Suvla Bay shore. His fighting days were few, but for several years he had prepared for the fray. Passing from the Holywell company of the Church Lads' Brigade, he joined the Holywell company of the 5th Battalion Royal Welch Fusiliers, and from private he was promoted gradually to sergeant. He was popular in his company, and everyone had a good word and admiration of him, as a smart intelligent soldier. He was the son of the late Mr. Harold Wallworth, and Mrs. Wallworth, New Road, Holywell, and was 22 years of age. A letter received by Mrs. Wallworth is worthy of mention. Mrs. Ada M. Shaw, of High Street, Royston, where the 5th were billeted for some time, writes on the 1st September:—"We have heard from the Dardanelles this morning, and it is with the deepest regret that we hear of the sad loss of poor Leslie. He was a friend of the two boys we had billeted with us, and spent all his spare time here, and all day on Sunday. You may have heard him mention us, as our children were all very fond of him. He used to sit and draw so nicely for them. We have saved all his letters and drawings. Three out of my four boys who were here are wounded. Is it not terrible, this awful murder of our brave boys? Hugh Davies from Bagillt wrote to us. He saw poor Leslie killed, but saw nothing more of him. He says he feels his loss so much. I trust God will give you strength to bear up under this terrible bereavement, and try to think of the dear boy as at rest in a hero's grave after nobly doing his duty." (Photo, Chettle, Rushden.)

Flintshire Observer 9th September 1915

The 1901 Census for Wales showing the Wallworth Family

Private Edwin Williams 21538
8th Battalion Manitoba Regiment

Edwin Williams was born in Holywell, Flintshire on 6th February 1888. His Parents were Robert Williams born in 1859 in Brynford, Flintshire and Hana Williams (nee Evans) born in 1860 in Gronant, Flintshire.

The 1901 census shows that the family lived in Lily Terrace, Brynford, Flintshire. Robert aged 42 was a Postman in Holywell, Hanna aged 41, his Wife and their six Children, Edwin, aged 14, William aged 12, Robert aged 9, Myfanwy aged 7, John aged 4 and Henry aged 2.

Edwin was educated at Brynford School and on leaving, obtained employment at W. Williams Printing Works, High Street, Holywell and then at Holywell Post Office, where his Father worked.

In the 1911 census it shows that he was living at the Talacre Stables, Prestatyn and was working as a Groom.

On Wednesday 28th September 1914 he enlisted in the Canadian Over-Seas Expeditionary Force (Saskatoon Fusiliers) at Camp Valcartier MRC De La Jaques-Cartier, Quebec and joined the 8th Battalion Manitoba Regiment.

He is described on his attestation papers as 5'6 ½" fair complextion, brown eyes, brown hair and fit for military service. He went thorough training on Sailsbury Plain. He travelled with the Regiment to France and served there and also in Flanders Belgium. He died of his wounds at a casuallty clearing station on Sunday 25th April 1915. His younger Brother William died 1st December 1918 serving with the Royal Defence Corps.

This notice appeared in the Flintshire Observer on 13th May 1915.

"Last Saturday morning Mr & Mrs Robert Williams, of the Calcot Arms Public House, Holywell, received sad news. A telegram was delivered stating – Regret to inform you that 21538 Private E Williams, 8th Battalion Canadian Infantry, has been killed"

He is commemorated on the Menin Gate Memorial, Ypres, Panel 24-26-28-30

- To find out more about Edwin Williams 8th Battalion Manitoba Regiment see chapter 4 of this book
-

Canadian Service Record Cards

Sailed from Quebec [...] on Royal Edward [...]

MARRIED	SINGLE	✓	WIDOWER

TRADE OR CALLING: Chauffeur   RELIGION: Church of England

DESCRIPTION

APPARENT AGE: 26 YEARS 6 MONTHS
HEIGHT: 3 FEET 6 INCHES
CHEST MEASUREMENT: 34 1/2 INCHES   EXPANSION: 1 1/2 INCHES
COMPLEXION: Fair   EYES: Brown   HAIR: Brown
DISTINGUISHING MARKS: 4 Vacc marks L. arm

MEDICAL EXAMINATION. PLACE: Valcartier, P.Q.   DATE: Aug 30th 1914

Present address Not Stated

No. 21538   RANK: Tr.   NAME: Williams E.

T.O.S.   UNIT: 105th Regt (Saskatoon Fusiliers)

M.D. 10

PAID FROM	PAID TO	SIG. OR REG'T	PROMOTIONS, TRANSFERS, DISCHARGES, ETC.	
			PARTICULARS	AUTHORITY
1914 Aug 12	1914 Aug 27	✓	Now shown on 11th Bn payroll	Sept payroll
Sept 27	Oct 31	✓		

UNIT SAILED
OCT 3 1914

LIST No.	HOSPITAL	DATE OF ADMISSION	REMARKS
34	Rep. from Base	16-4-15	Wounded 16-4-15.
52	Rep. Date by telegram	8-5-15	Killed in Action
198.3	correct date of death	25-4-15	

NAME: Williams, E.
H. Q. FILE No. 649-
REGT'L. No. 21538
RANK AND CORPS: Pte. 8th Battalion (formerly 11th Batt.)

CABLE NO.	DATE	NATURE OF CASUALTY
C.277	23/4/15	Wounded Apl. 16th.
C.829	8/5/15	Killed in Action
L.F.B.2090a.		Killed in Action at Ypres. Apr 25, 1915

NO./6/2
+FOLL.

Canadian Service Record Cards

Plaque on St. James' Parish Church wall, Holywell

Private Edwin Williams, 8th Battalion Canadians (eldest son of Mr. Robert Williams, Holywell), who, as reported last week, has been killed in action.

Flintshire Observer 20th May 1915

St. John's Cathedral Memorial, Saskatoon, Canada on which Edwin William's name appears

This Memorial is located just west of the Saskatchewa Legislative Building in Regina, near Wascana Lake and the Albert Memorial Bridge.

Saskatchewan World War One Memorial was dedicated in 1995 in memory of 5,348 young men and women from Saskatchewan who were killed in the First World War

Lieutenant Hugh Osborne Williams
"C" Company 5th Battalion Royal Welsh Fusiliers

Hugh Osborne Williams was born on the 31st of July 1877 in Bodgwyn House, Brynford Street, Holywell.

The 1881 census has the family living at Bodgwyn House, Brynford Street, Holywell.

The Head of the family was Joseph Williams aged 40, who was a Civil & Mining Engineer, his Wife Elizabeth Ellen aged 44 and their Nine children, Arthur Caradoc aged 15, an apprentice Civil Engineer, Edward John Herbert aged 14, Joseph Llewellyn aged 13, Albert Foster aged 11, Peter Ernest Henry aged 10, Frances Ellen aged 8, Ivor Owen aged 6, Hugh Osborne aged 3, William Neville Pennant aged 1. Also living with the family at the time was Hannah Matthews aged 17, who was employed as a General Domestic Servant.

The 1911 census stated that the family now lived at Tros-y-Maes, Holywell. The Head of the family was Elizabeth Ellen Williams aged 74 a widow. Joseph, her Husband, had died a few years earlier. There were two Sons still living at home, Hugh Osborne Williams aged 33 who was employed as an Analytic Chemist and William Neville Pennant Williams aged 30 a Medical Student. One of the other Sons Albert Foster Williams still lived in Holywell and was a Founder Member of the Baskingwerk Masonic Lodge, later becoming Master of the Lodge in 1918.

Hugh Osborne Williams enlisted as a Commissioned Officer (2nd Lieutenant) in the 5th Battalion Royal Welsh Fusiliers on the 4th of June 1913. He was previously a Sergeant in the 5th Battalion. His height is recorded as 5'6" and was still living at Tros-y-Maes in Holywell and employed as a Chemist.

Hugh Osborne Williams died of his wounds on the 12th of August 1915 aged 38 at Gallipoli. He is remembered on the Helles Memorial Gallipoli. Panel 77 to 80.

He is also remembered on the North Wales Heroes' Memorial Arch in Bangor.

- **To find out more about Hugh Osborne Williams 5th Battalion Royal Welsh Fusiliers see chapter 4 of this book**

Photograph Thanks to Peter Metcalf

Hugh Osborne Williams in his Flint United football kit

Plaque on St. James' Parish Church wall, Holywell &

Helles Memorial, Gallipoli

From 9/Gazette/8782

5th (Flintshire) Battalion, The Royal Welsh Fusiliers.

The undermentioned non-commissioned officers to be Second Lieutenants. Dated

Serjeant Hugh Osborne Williams

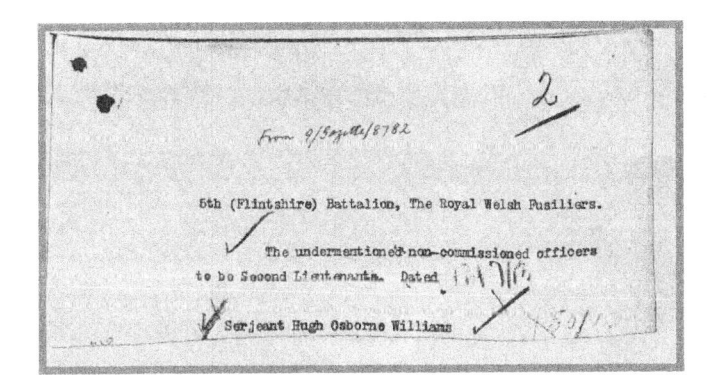

This is Hugh Osborne Williams' Application for Promotion from Sargeant to Second Lieutenant June 4th 1913

Army Form E. 536.

QUESTIONS TO BE ANSWERED BY A CANDIDATE FOR APPOINTMENT TO A COMMISSION IN THE TERRITORIAL FORCE.

N.B.—It is of great importance, especially in the case of Candidates for the Regular Forces, that the names given in the Birth Certificate should be correctly stated on this form, and it is to be clearly understood that, where they differ, the names and date of Birth given on the Birth or Baptismal Certificates will be accepted for Official record. The attention of General Officers Commanding-in-Chief is invited to War Office letter of the 28th March, 1907, No. 106/6 (C.R.A.I.)

Regiment or Corps for which recommended	Royal Welsh Fus
If more than one Battalion Regt., for which Battalion recommended	5th Battalion
Rank to which to be appointed	2nd Lieutenant
1. Are you a British subject by birth or naturalization?	yes
2. Are you of pure European descent?	yes
3. What is your full Surname?	Williams
4. What are your full Christian names? (See "N.B." above)	Hugh Osborne
*5. What is the exact date of your birth? (See "N.B." above)	31st 1877
6. What is your height?	five feet six inches
7. Where were you born?	Holywell, Flintshire
8. At what school or college were you educated?	
9. What is your address for correspondence?	
10. What is your profession or occupation?	Chemist
11. Do you now hold a Commission, or are you now serving in any of His Majesty's Regular, Reserve, Territorial, Auxiliary, Indian or Colonial Forces, the Channel Islands Militia, or the Officers Training Corps? If so, state the nature of the commission you hold, or the capacity in which you are serving.	Sergeant 5th R.W.F.
12. Have you held a Commission in, or have you served in any of His Majesty's Regular, Reserve, Territorial, Auxiliary, Indian or Colonial Forces, the Channel Islands Militia, or the Officers Training Corps?	yes
If so, state:—	
a. The Regiment or Corps to which you served.	5th R.W.F.
b. If commissioned, the date of the resignation of your commission.	no
c. Your rank on retirement.	still serving
d. If not commissioned, the date of your discharge.	—
e. The circumstances in which you retired, or were discharged; and	—
f. Whether you have served in any campaign. If you have, attach a statement certified by a Senior Officer who is personally cognizant of such service.	no
13. Have you been nominated for any other Regiment or Corps?	no

I certify the above answers to be correct.

Usual Signature of Candidate.   H. O. Williams

Date   June 4th 1913

MEDICAL CERTIFICATE.

I certify that _Hugh O Williams_ is fit in health for the discharge of the duties of an Officer of the Territorial Force.

Signature   H. W. Williams

Date   4th June 1913

* Does not apply to a candidate who has served as a Commissioned Officer in the Regular Army, the Territorial Force, or the British Auxiliary Forces.

[see over.

Army Form B. 2090A.

FIELD SERVICE

REPORT of Death of an Officer to be forwarded to the War Office with the least possible delay after receipt of notification of death on Army Form B. 213, or Army Form A. 36, or from other official documentary sources.

UNIT: 1/5th. Battalion Royal Welsh Fusiliers.

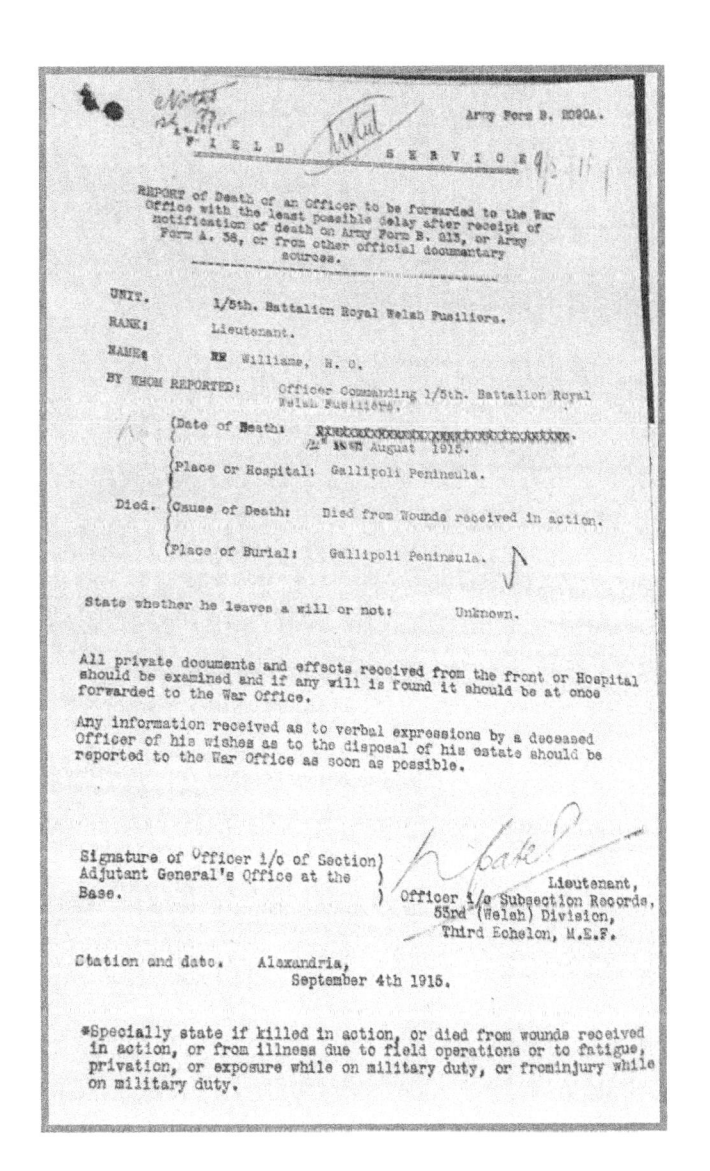

RANK: Lieutenant.

NAME: Williams, H. O.

BY WHOM REPORTED: Officer Commanding 1/5th. Battalion Royal Welsh Fusiliers.

Died.
- (Date of Death: ~~xxxxxxxxxxxxxxxxxxxxxxxxxx~~ /2" 18th August 1915.
- (Place or Hospital: Gallipoli Peninsula.
- (Cause of Death: Died from Wounds received in action.
- (Place of Burial: Gallipoli Peninsula.

State whether he leaves a will or not: Unknown.

All private documents and effects received from the front or Hospital should be examined and if any will is found it should be at once forwarded to the War Office.

Any information received as to verbal expressions by a deceased Officer of his wishes as to the disposal of his estate should be reported to the War Office as soon as possible.

Signature of Officer i/c of Section)
Adjutant General's Office at the   )   Lieutenant,
Base.   )   Officer i/c Subsection Records,
                                            53rd (Welsh) Division,
                                            Third Echelon, M.E.F.

Station and date. Alexandria, September 4th 1915.

*Specially state if killed in action, or died from wounds received in action, or from illness due to field operations or to fatigue, privation, or exposure while on military duty, or from injury while on military duty.

This is a Field Service Note, to be forwarded to the War Office informing them of the death of Lieutenant Hugh Osborne Williams

Private Joseph Edward Williams 28451
4th Battalion South Wales Borderers

Joseph Edward Williams was born in Holywell in 1898.

The 1901 census shows the family resided in Holywell. Head of the family was Thomas E. Williams aged 30, he was a Grocer's Assistant, his Wife Sarah aged 26 and their three Children, Mary aged 4, Joseph Edward aged 3 and John Llewellyn aged 1.

The 1911 census shows the family still living in Holywell, at the Grapes House, High Street. Thomas E. Williams was now a Grocer, Sarah his Wife aged 36 and their Children Mary aged 14, Joseph Edward aged 13 and Thomas Llewellyn aged 10 and also further Children Lilian aged 9, Gwendoline aged 5, Thomas aged 7 and Lewis aged 1.

Joseph Edward Williams previously served with the Royal Welsh Fusiliers, service number 2653 and then transferred to the South Wales Borderers.

Joseph Edward Williams was killed in action on the 15th February 1917 aged 19 and is buried in the Amara War Cemetery in Iraq.

His Widowed Mother was shown as living in 2 Bank Place, High Street, Holywell when the pension correspondance was sent.

- **To find out more about Joseph Edward Williams, 4th Battalion South Wales Borderers see chapter 4 of this book**

Amara War Cemetery Iraq & Plaque on St. James'
Parish Church wall, Holywell

Joseph Edward Williams Medal Card

The Grapes where Joseph Ewdard Williams lived (now an Iceland store)

Private John Llewellyn Williams 77222
13th Battalion Royal Welsh Fusiliers

John Llewellyn Williams was born in Holywell in 1900.

In the 1901 census, the family lived in Holywell. Head of the family was Thomas E. Williams aged 30 who was a Grocer's Assistant, his Wife Sarah aged 26 and their Children Mary aged 4, Joseph Edward aged 3 and John Llewellyn aged 1.

In the 1911 census, the family still lived in Holywell, at Grape House High Street, Holywell. Thomas E. Williams aged 40 was now a Grocer, sarah his Wife aged 36 and their Children Mary aged 14, Joseph Edward aged 13, John Llewellyn aged 10, Lilian aged 9, Gewndoline aged 5, Thomas aged 7 and Lewis aged 1.

John was killed in action on the 29th August 1918 and is listed on the Vis-En-Artois Memorial Pas De Calais, France. His older Brother Joseph Edward Williams was also killed in action in 1917.

His widowed Mother was shown as living in 2 Bank Place, High Street, Holywell when she requested a pension from the army.

- **To find out more about John Llewellyn Williams, 13th Battalion Royal Welsh Fusiliers Regiment see chapter 4 of this book**

John Llewellyn Williams' Vis-En-Artois Memorial, Pas De Calais Panel 6

Plaque on St. James' Parish Church wall, Holywell

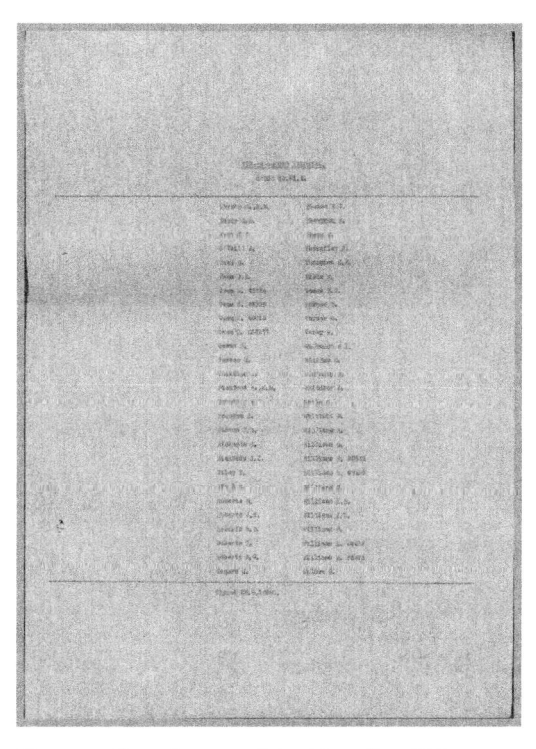

The panel list showing John Llewellyn Williams at the Ais-En-Artois Memorial

Corporal Mesech Williams 14672
10th Battalion Royal Welsh Fusiliers

Mesech Williams was born in Holywell in 1891.

The 1911 census states that the family recided at 1 St. Winifreds Terrace, New Road, Holywell. The Head of the family was Thomas Williams aged 49, a Colliery Hewer, his Wife Rebecca aged 46 and their three Sons, Thomas aged 23, A Labourer, Mesech, aged 20 a Shop Assistant and William aged 18, a General Labourer. William was also killed in the First World War.

On 7th June 1915 Mesech enlisted with the 10th Battalion Royal Welsh Fusiliers at the Drill Hall, Halkyn Street, Holywell.

Mesech arrived in France with the Battalion on 27th September 1915.

Mesech was killed in action on 20th July 1916 during the Battle for Delville Wood, during the Somme Campaign and is buried at Delville Wood Cemetery, Longueval, Plot: XV. Row: K. Grave: 6

Mesech is also remembered on the North Wales Heroes' Memorial Arch in Bangor.

- **To find out more about Mesech Williams, 10th Battalion Royal Welsh Fusiliers see chapter 4 of this book**

Plaque on St. James Parish Church wall, Holywell

Deville Wood Cemetery Longueval, Plot: XV. Row: K. Grave: 6

*Authors own photograph

Mesech Willimas Medal Index Card

Private William Williams 14645
16th Battalion Royal Welsh Fusiliers

William Williams was born in Holywell in 1893.

The 1901 census has the family living at St. Winifreds Terrace, New Road, Holywell. Head of the family was Thomas Williams aged 41, employed as a Collier, his Wife, Rebecca aged 36 and their 9 Children, Robert aged 16, Edward aged 14, Thomas aged 12, Mesech aged 9, William aged 8, Harriet aged 7, Stephen aged 5, John aged 4 and Hanna aged 2.

The 1911 census has the family still living at St. Winifreds Terrace, New Road, Holywell. Head of the family is Thomas Williams aged 51, A Collier, Rebecca aged 46, and their Childern Thomas aged 23 A Labourer, Mesech aged 20 a Shop Assistant, William aged 18, a General Labourer, Harriet aged 17 A Weaver, Stephen aged 15 a Splicer at the Cotton Mill, John aged 14, a Porter at the Drapery Shop, Hanna aged 12, Margaret aged 9, Edwin aged 7, Eunice aged 5.

William served with the 16th Battalion Royal Welsh Fusiliers and was killed in action on 17th May 1918 during the Battle of Awely Wood, Somme, France. He is buried at Bouzincourt Communal Cemetery Extension, Plot III, Row C, Grave 8. His Brother Mesech was also killed in the First World War.

William in also remembered on the North Wales Heroes' Memorial Arch in Bangor.

- To read more about William Williams' 16th Battalion Royal Welsh Fusiliers see Chapter 4 of this book

William Williams is buried at Bouzincourt Communal Cemetery Extension, Plto 111, Row C, Grave 8

WILLIAM WILLIAMS.
PTE. 16 BATT. R.W.F.
MAY 17TH, 1918.
FRANCE.

Plaque on St. James Parish Church wall in Holywell

Rebecca dec'd.

CLAIMANT.   M.P.W. 5.

Surname WILLIAMS.   Registered No. 5/D/7450.
(Block Letters)

Christian Name Thomas.

Man's Name 1 WILLIAMS Mesech
            2 WILLIAMS William
(Surname first: in block letters)

Regimental / Official No. 1 14672
                           2 14645
Rank / Rating 1 acpl
               2 Pte

Regiment / Ship ½ RWFus.   Relationship to Man   Father

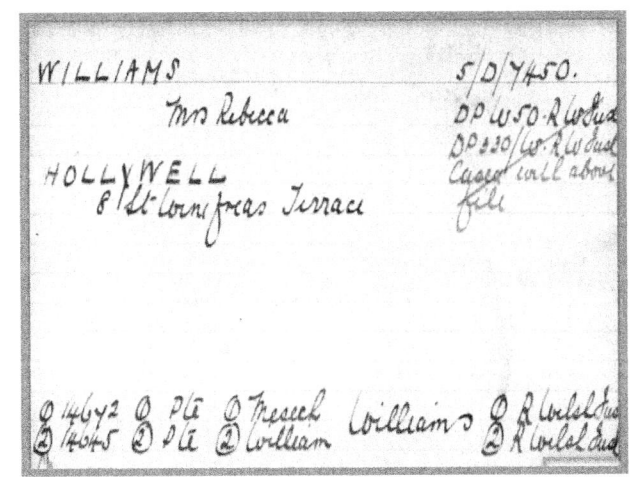

WILLIAMS   5/D/7450.
    Mrs Rebecca
HOLLYWELL
  8 St Winifreds Terrace

Mother of William and his Brother Mesech Williams

Pension Claims Cards

Lance Sergeant William Williams 240284 (46864)

5th Battalion Royal Welsh Fusiliers & Royal Defence Corps

Williams Williams was born on 3rd March 1889, Brynford, Flintshire.

His Parent's were Robert William born 1859 and Hanna Williams (nee Evans) born 1860.

The 1901 census shows the family living in Lily Terrace, Brynford, Flintshire. Robert, aged 42 was a Postman in Holywell, Hanna Williams aged 41 and six Children, Edwin aged 14, William aged 12, Robert aged 9, Myfanwy aged 7, John aged 4 and Hanna aged 2.

William left school and eventually became a School Master at Bagillt County School.

On the 20th April 1914 he married Harriet Mabel Taylor of the Dolphin Inn, Whitford Street, Holywell.

William enlisted with the Royal Welsh Fusiliers and later transferred to the Royal Defence Corps.

He was admitted to the Military Hospital, Oswestry where he died on 1st December 1918, most likely from influenza.

His older Brother Edwin, also listed on the Memorial in Holywell, was killed in April 1915.

William was buried at St. Michael's Churchyard, Brynford, Holywell.

- To read about William Williams Royal Defence Corps, see Chapter 4 of this book

St. Michael's Graveyard, Brynford, Holywell

*Authors own photograph

Plaque on St. James' Parish Church wall, Holywell

SEC T. W. WILLIAMS.
1/5. R.W.F. DEC. 1ST. 1918.
MILITARY HOSPITAL.
OSWESTRY.

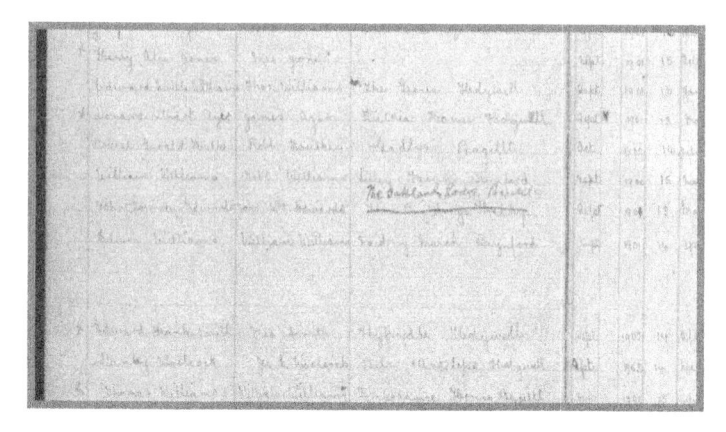

William Williams School Entry Record to Holywell County School

Holywell County School, where William attended

Private Benjamin Walker 68423 (later 44897)

King's Liverpool Regiment 10 COY Transferred to the Labour Corps

Benjamin Walker was born in 1878 in Holywell, Flintshire.

The 1881 census shows the Head of the family was John Walker aged 28 who worked as a Cooper, a maker of wooden casks/barrels/buckets etc, his Wife Elizabeth Walker aged 28 and their Children William Thomas aged 3 and Benjamin aged 2, they lived in Summer Hill, Holywell.

The 1891 census shows the family now living at New Road, Holywell. John, the Head of the family was now 38 and still worked as a Cooper. His Wife Elizabeth aged 38 now had six Children. William Thomas aged 13, Benjamin aged 12, Margaret aged 8, Andrew aged 6, Joseph aged 3 and Mary aged 8 months.

The 1901 census has Benjamin aged 22 working as a Groom at a house called "Sand Hey" in Holylake, Cheshire. The house was owned by the Timber Merchant, Arthur Dempsey, who was 77. Mr Dempsey lived there with his Wife and two grown up Children. The family employed five Servants, which included Benjamin Walker.

In 1906 Benjamin married Elanor Edward Lees in the Parish Church, Nannerch, Flintshire. Their Son John was born in 1907 and their Daughter Mary Elizabeth in 1909.

The 1911 census shows the family living at Oakfield Lodge, Stapley, Nantwich, Benjamin aged 32 was a Coachman, his Wife Eleanor, also aged 32 and his Children John aged 4 and Mary Elizabeth aged 2. The family had a third child, Reginald, born in 1916.

Benjamin was conscripted into the Army on the 24th February 1917, he was 40 years old. He was still married and still worked as a Coachman. He served at home (in Britain), until 11th March 1917. He joined the British Expeditionary Force in France on 12th March 1917 and served abroad until his death on 13th February 1918. Although his original service was with the 10th Labour Battalion of the Kings Liverpool Regiment, he served most of his active service with the 75th COY Labour Corps.

The Army records contain internal memos reporting his death which had occurred at 3.45pm on the 13th February 1918 at 64 Casualty Clearing Station in Proven, Belgium. He died of Nephritis (inflamation of the kidneys) while on active service. This was known as "Trench Nephritis". 35,000 British and 2000 American troops suffered from Nephritis during the First World War, the poor conditions proving to be a factor in this condition.

Benjamin is buried at Mendinghem Military Cemetery, near Poperinge, Belgium. Benjamin is also remembered on a Memorial at St. Martin's, Ashton On Mersey.

- **To read more of Benjamin Walker's Kings Liverpool Regimant 10 COY see Chapter 4 of this book**

Letter confirming where the personal effects of Private Benjamin Walker should be sent to

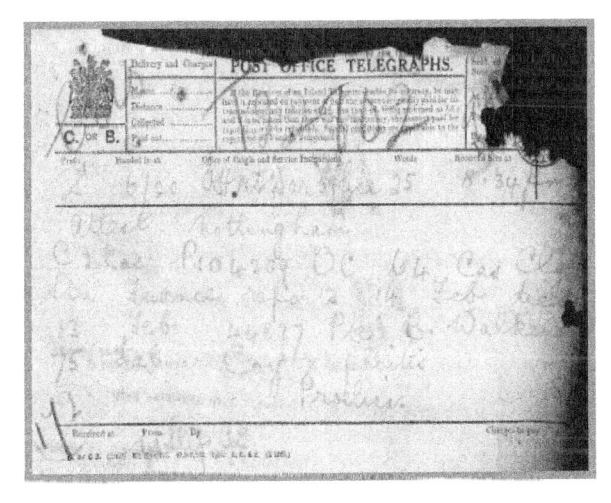

Telegram informing the family of the death of Private Benjamin Walker

Mendinghem Military Cemetery IX. D. 20

Oakfield House, Nantwich where Benjamin Walker lived and worked as a Coachman

Chapter 4
The Battalions In Which They Served

This chapter is about the story of the Battalions that the men listed on the Holywell Memorial served with during the confilct. This chapter is a brief description into each of the Battalions.

The Royal Welch Fusiliers are one of the oldest Regiments in the regular Army, hence the archaic spelling of the word "Welch" instead of "Welsh". In the Boar War and throughout the First World War, the Army officially called the Regimant "The Royal Welsh Fusiliers" but the archaic "Welch" was officially restored to the Regiments title in 1920 under Army Order No. 56.

1st Battalion Royal Welsh Fusiliers

The 1st Battalion The Royal Welsh Fusiliers were in Malta when the war broke out in August 1914. They returned to England, landing in Southampton on 3rd September 1914, they joined 22nd Brigade 7th Division based in the New Forrest, Hampshire. The Division left for Belgium on the 7th October 1914 landing at Zeebrugge to assist with the Defence of Antwerp. They arrived too late to prevent the fall of the city and took up defensive positions at importnant bridges and intersections, to aid the retreat of the Belgium Army. The 7th Division were the first British troops to entrench in the Front of Ypres, suffering heavy losses, in what was to be known as "The First Battle of Ypres". By February 1915, the Division had been brought back up to fighting strength and they saw action at the Battle of Neuve Chapelle, the Battle of Aubers, the Battle of Festubert, the Second Action of Givenchy and the Battle of Loos.

In 1917 the Division fought during the German retreat to the Hindenburg Line and the Flanking Operations around Ballecourt during the Arras Offensive, before returning to Flanders for the Third Battle of Ypres, seeing action in the Battle Of Polygon Wood, the Battle of Broodseinde, the Battle of Poelcapelle and the Second Battle of Passchendaele.

In late 1917, the 7th Division moved to Italy taking up positions along the river Paive. The Division played a pivital role in the crossing the river Piave in January 1918.

Siegfried Sassoon, the famous War Poet, serving with the Sussex Yeomanry at the outbreak of the First World War, was commissioned into the 3rd Battalion (Special Reserve) Royal Welsh Fusiliers, as a Second Lieutenant on the 29th May 1915. In November 1915 Sassoon was sent to the 1st Battalion Royal Weslh Fusiliers serving in France.

Sassoon's service on the Western Front were marked by exceptionally brave actions and he was awarded the Military Cross. He was nicknamed "Mad Jack" by his men for his near suicidal exploits.

Poem called "Absolution" by Siefried Sassoon (1886-1967)

The anguish of the earth absolves our eyes
Till beauty shines in all that we can see
War is our scourge, yet war has made us wise
And fighting for our freedom, we are free

-

Horror of wounds and anger at the foe
And loss of things desired, all these must pass
We are the happy legion, for we know
Time's but a golden wind that shakes the grass

-

There was an hour where we were loth to part
From life we longed to share no less than others
Now, having claimed this heritage of heart
What need we more, my comrades and my brothers?

Siegfried Sassoon during the war

2nd Battalion Royal Welsh Fusiliers

The 2nd Battalion Royal Welsh Fusiliers were in Portland when War broke out in August 1914.

They proceeded to France on the 11th August 1914 landing in Rouen, they became attached to the 19th Infantry Brigade. The Brigade transferred to the 6th Division on the 12t October 1914 then on the 31st May 1915 they transferred to the 27th Division and in August transferred to the 2nd Division and in November 1915 transferred to the 33rd Division.

In 1916 the Battalion saw action on the Somme. In 1917 the Battle of Arras and the Hindenburg Line then moved to Flanders for the Thrid Battle of Ypres.

On the 6th February 1918 they transferred to 115th Brigade, 38th (Welsh) Division and fought in battles on the Somme and the final advance in Picardy.

One of the soldiers who served with the 2nd Battalion Royal Welsh Fusiliers was the famous Poet Robert Graves

Graves gained a commission in the Royal Welsh Fusiliers in 1914 and served in France from 1915, fighting in the Battle of Loos and the Battle of the Somme. Graves was severley injured at the Battle of High Wood and was infact, given up for dead, but survived having being buried, only when one of the soldiers noticed he was still breathing. His Parents even received a letter informing them of his death. One day later, they received another letter from Graves himself informing them that he is getting better!

Sent home, Graves spent some of his time in 1918 at Kimmel Camp and spent his leave walking along the river at Rhuddlan, near the castle.

He wrote of his military experiences in "Goodbye To All That", this is one of his poems from that book;

The Last Post

The bugler sent a call of high romance -
"Lights out! Lights out", to the deserted square.
On the thin brazen notes he threw a prayer,
"God, if it's this for me next time in France…
O spare the phantom bugle as I lie,
Dead in the gas and smoke and roar of guns,
Dead in a row with other broken ones,
Lying so stiff and still under the sky,
Jolly young fusiliers too good to die".

Robert Graves during the War

3rd (Reserve) Battalion Royal Welsh Fusiliers

The 3rd (Reserve) Battalion Royal Welsh Fusiliers, in August 1914 whose headquarters were in Wrexham, but physically based in Pembroke Dock. The 3rd Battalion was a training unit, it remained in the UK throughout the War but moved to Litherland near Liverpool in May 1915, moved to Ireland in November 1917 and by the time the end of the War, they were based in Limerick.

3rd (Reserve) Battalion Royal Welsh Fusiliers at Litherland 1915

1/5th Battalion Royal Welsh Fusiliers

The 5th Battalion Flintshire Territorials were part of the North Wales Infantry Brigade, under the overall command of Colonel F. C. Lloyd, formed in 1860 from local volunteers.

5th Battlion Royal Welsh Fusiliers departed from Flint on 22nd August 1914 in "High Spirits" for Northampton, where they marched through the streets the following day. The 5th were stationed at Rushdon and Higham Ferrars until 21st December when they moved to Cambridgeshire. On the 5th May 1915 they moved to Bedford where on the 15th of May they become part of the 53rd (Welsh) Territorial Division, under the command of Major General Hon. J. E. Lindley. The Division was divided into three Brigades, the 5th Battalion was assigned to 158th Brigade which consisted of 4 Battalions. The 5th commanded by Lieutenant Colonel Basil Edwin Philips.

The 5th Battalion boarded trains on the 13th July at Irchester and the next day embarked from Devenport on the S.S. Caledonia.

On the 17th, the ship docked at Gibralter and the next day entered the Mediterranean. Arriving at Alexanderia on the 25th July a couple of days later.

The Battalion disembarked at Mudros Bay, on the Greek Island of Lemnos.

For the following week, they continued training.

On the 8th of August 29 Officers (including a Chaplin and Medical Officer) and all other ranks boarded the H. M. S. Rowan.

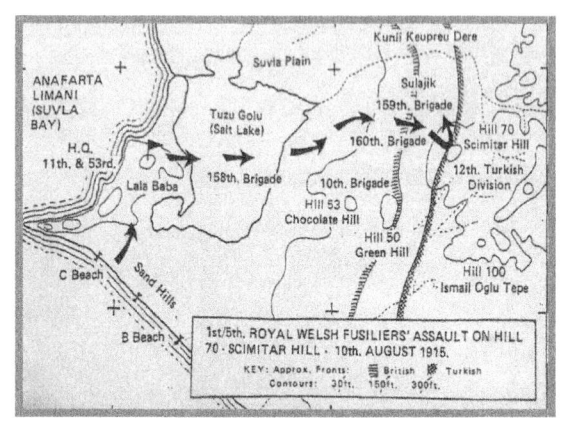

They sailed to the Island of Imbros, where they anchored for the night. The next morning, they sailed at 4.30am towards Suvla Bay landing at C Beach around 6am. The 5th were the first to disembark in small boats, as dawn approached, they started taking enemy fire from the Turks and were forced to leave the beach to find cover in land, making camp at Lala Baba.

On the 10th August, Reveille was 0.330am. the Officers having been told the previous evening that the 5th would be moving inland to engage the enemy. Thet were to act as a reserve to the 159th Brigade until they reached the area of Sulajik and then continue an attack agaist the Anfarta Spur, which should, at the time, be under bombardment. At 0.445am the 158th Brigade moved from Lala Baba with the 5th Flintshire in the centre and leading the advance with the 7th on the right and the 6th on the left, together with the 2nd/10th Middlesex.

The first obstacle the 5th came to was a large semi-dry Salt-lake which consisted of 2 miles of mud, covered with a white salt crust. One soldier later described it as being on the sands on the River Dee between Flint and Neston. No sooner had they begun to cross the Salt-lake, a Taube Spotter Plane reported their position to the Turkish Artillary on the hills three miles away. When they were half way across the Salt-lake, the 5th experienced their first bombardment, which caused some casulaties. Captain Armstrong of D Company, was the first to be wounded, when sharpnel hit him in the leg. Private Robert Hayes, a member of the Machine Gun Team, was hit by shrapnel to his face. The wounded men managed to either make their own way back to the landing beach or were helped by the Stretcher Bearers.

When the Battalion, led by A Company reached the edge of the Salt-lake, they came under gunfire from the South East. Captain Beswick led the Leading Company in Skirmishing formation, while the rest had spread out and were moving forward at short ditances at a time until they reached the brush beyond the lake. The two Leading Companies took the full brunt of the enemy machine gun and rifle fire, which was coming from Hill 50, but they managed to reach Sulajik without great loss.

They were then ordered to advance on Scimitar Hill, in attempt to capture this important target, they would have to succeed, where the previous day's attempt had failed. The men of the 5th could see the hill was burnt and littered with dead from both sides.

Colonel Philips led his men beyond the trenches and sent the following message to Colonel James of the 1st/6th Royal Welsh Fusiliers,

"Bring all the men you can find to where I am, 200 yards in the front of 159th Brigade trenches. We can rush the hill they are shelling, as soon as they stop".

The Colonel of the 6th had become seperated from the main body of his men.

The order to "Fix Bayonets" was given, Colonel Phillips moved up the and down the line encouraging his men "Come on Boys! Come On the Fighting Fifth".

As the shelling of the Turkish trenches had stopped, one observer, watching the attack from Chocolate Hill described a mass of Khaki Figures rushing up the hill in a fan-shaped formation, the terrain was diffcult to traverse and soon the attack was split up into small groups. When the attack reached within 150 yards of the Turkish trenches, the Turks evacuated their trench and it looked like the 5th were going to take the objective, but the Turkish Artillary opened up with a very accurate and devastating heavy bombardment. Colonel Phillips, leading the men to a great victory neared th top of the ridge, was hit and died instantly.

Colonel Basil E Philips

Some of the 5th reached the trenches, whilst others almost reached the top of the hill before being forced to take cover.

The heavy bombardment continued and many of the troops were compelled to retreat. Seeing the situatuon, the Turks returned to their trenches and some hand-to-hand combat took place. Once the Turks had regained their trenches, they began to enfilade the British with machine gun and rifle fire. The attack had started at 11.30am but by 1300 hours, the assault had failed. There were many casualties and now the Battalion was mixed up with Dublin Fusiliers, Lancashire and Yorkshire Regiments. The attack on Scimitar Hill had failed. The Flintshire men had suffered their "Baptism of Fire". The 5th had their Commanding Officer, 4 Officers and 13 other ranks killed. One Officer and 39 other ranks, missing (presumed killed). 6 Officers and 116 other ranks had been wounded.

By the time the Battalion were evacuated to the Mudros on the 11th December 1915, the Division stood at just 162 Officers and 2,428 men, approx 15% of it's original strength.

From Mudros they went onto Alexandria and to Wardan.

The 5th Battalion were in action at the Battle of Romani in the Palenstine Campaign in 1916, and in 1917 fought in the First Battle of Gaza, Second Battle of Gaza, and in the Third Battle of Gaza they captured Beersheba, Tell Khuweilfe and the capture of Jerusalem.

In March 1918, they fought in the Balle of Tell'asur.

On the 3rd August 1918 the Battalion amalgamated with the 1st/6th Battalion to form 5th/6th Battalion.

OFFICERS OF THE 5TH BATTALION, ROYAL WELSH FUSILIERS (T.F.)

From left to right are: Back row: Captain T. H. Armstrong (wounded), Lieut. H. M. Davies (wounded), Lieut. D. R. K. Roberts, Lieut. Jenkins, Lieut. R. M. Mocatta (missing), Lieut. F. Kenny, Lieut. A. N. Acbury (wounded); middle row— —; Lieut. Garrison, Captain A. Kingsbury (wounded), Captain H. A. Jefferson, Lieut. H. Berwick, —; front row— Captain J. E. Parry, Captain T. H. Parry (wounded), Major W. Borthwick, Lieut.-Colonel B. E. Philipps (killed), Captain Lang, Captain W. Berwick, —

5th Battalion Royal Welch Fusiliers, Higham Ferrers, 1915.

to r. *Front row*: Capt. G. Morgan, M.O. Dr. P. E. Hook, Chaplain, Captain G. Claridge, Q.M., Maj. W
Maj. B. Head, Lt. Col. Phillips, Capt. Borthwick, Capt. Tricket, Capt. T. Parry, M.P., Capt. J. E
d row: Lt. Ashley, Capt. E. Roberts, Lt. Synnot, Capt. M Davies, Lt. K. Roberts, Mocatta, Lt. T. Bate, L
Lt. Kenney, Capt. Armstrong, Capt. H. A. Jerretson, Lt. King, Lt. Jenkins, Capt. Taylor
Back row: Lt. H. Williams, Lt. P. Dealtry, Lt. Alexander, Lt. Hughes, Capt. Kingsbury

(Pictured on the right is)

Father P. E. Hook – Chaplin for the 5th Battalion Royal Welsh Fusiliers

Hook was badly wounded at Gallipoli but survived the war

3rd/5th Battalion Royal Welsh Fusiliers

Formed in Flint in March 1915.

On the 8th April 1916 it became the 4th/7th Reserve Battalion.

1st September 1916 based with the Welsh Reserve Brigade at Oswestry and moved in March 1918 to Kimnel Camp, Rhyl and in July 1918 to Herne Bay, Kent.

Kimnel Camp 1916

1/6th Battalion Royal Welsh Fusiliers

1/6th Battalion (Caernarvoshire & Anglesey) Battalion formed in Caernarfon in August 1914, moved immediately on mobalisation to Conwy then moved to Northampton at the end of August, then to Coddenham in Suffolk on 30th November 1914, then to Walsham-Le-Willows on 13th December 1914, onto Cabbridge on the 9th January 1915 then moved to Beford in May 1915 where the formation became 158th Brigade 53rd Welsh Division. 19th July 1915 they sailed from Davenport on the Caledonia, sailing via Lemnos and Imbros. On the 9th August they disembarked at "C" Beach, Sulva Bay, Gallipoli. They fought on Gallipoli until December 1915 when they evacuated to Egypt.

The 6th Battalion were in action at the Battle of Romani in the Palenstine Campaign in 1916, and in 1917 fought in the First Battle of Gaza, Second Battle of Gaza, and in the Third Battle of Gaza they captured Beersheba, Tell Khuweilfe and the capture of Jerusalem.

In March 1918, they fought in the Balle of Tell'asur. On the 3rd August 1918 the 1st/6th Battalion amalgamated with 1/5th Battalion to form the 5/6th Battalion

"C" Beach Sulva Bay, Gallipoli, where the 6th Battalion landed on 9th August 1915

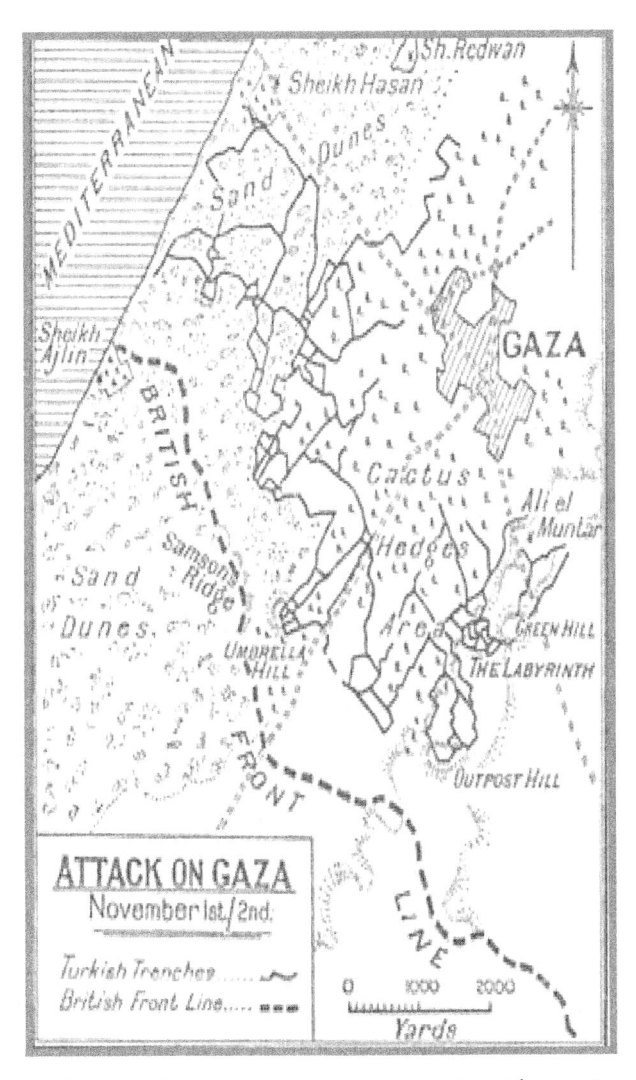

3rd Battle of Gaza, November 1917, where The 6th Battalion Royal Welsh Fusiliers Fought

10th (Service) Battalion Royal Welsh Fusiliers

The 10th (Service) Battalion Royal Welsh Fusiliers was raised at Wrexham on the 16th of October 1914 as part of Kitchener's Third New Army and joined 76th Brigade, 25th Division. They moved to Codford St. Mary for training and spent the winter in Billets in Bournemouth. The Battalion moved to Romsey on the 29th April 1915 and then onto Aldershot for final training on the 3rd of June 1915. They proceeded to France, landing at Boulogne on the 27th of September 1915. On the 15th October 1915 the Battalion transferred with 76th Brigade to the 3rd Division. They saw action at Railway Wood, near Ypres in 1916. They took part in the Action of the Bluff and St. Eloi Craters. They then moved to the Somme for the Battle of Albert, the Battle of Bazentine helping capture Longueval, the Battle of Delville Wood and the Battle on the Ancre.

In 1917 they fought at Arras and then the Battle of the Scarpe and the Battle of Arleux. They moved North to return to Flanders and were in action during the Battle of Menin Road and the Battle of Polygon Wood, during the Third Battle of Ypres. They then moved South and were in action at the Battle of Cambrai.

On the 8th of February 1918, when the Army was re-organised, the 10th Battalion disbanded in France, with the men transferring into the 8th Entrenching Battalion.

The 1914 British Wartime Recruitment Poster Depicting Lord Kitchener with The Words "Your Country Needs You"

The King And Lord Kitchener Inspecting The Troops At Aldershot August 1915 Before the 10th Battalion Royal Welsh Fusiliers Embarked for France

S.S. Onward Troop Ship That Carried The 10th Battalion Royal Welsh Fusiliers To France

13th (1st North Wales) Battalion Royal Welsh Fusiliers

The 13th (1st North Wales) Battalion Royal Welsh Fusiliers was raised at Rhyl on the 3rd September 1914 by the Denbigh and Flint Territorial Force Association. Transferred to the Welsh National Executive Committee on the 10th October and then in November 1914 they joined the 128th Brigade, 34th Division at Llandudno, which was renamed 113th Brigade, 38th (Welsh) Division on the 28th April 1915.

They moved to Winchester for the final training in August 1915 and proceeded to France in December 1915. In July 1916 they were in action at Mametz Wood on the Somme, suffering severe casualties. The Division did not return to major action for more than 12 months. In 1917 they were in action in the Third Battle of Ypres then in 1918, they were in action on the Somme, in the Battle of Hindenburg Line and the final advance in Picardy.

Demobilisation began in December 1918 and was completed by June 1919.

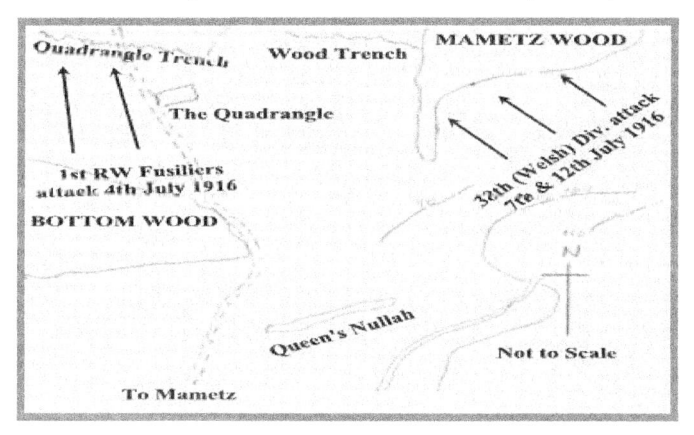

A Map Showing The Attack On Mametz Wood Which The 13th Battalion Were Part Of

Painting by Christopher Williams (1873-1934)

The Welsh Division at Mametz Wood, 1916

The Battle of Mametz Wood in July 1916 was part of the Somme Offensive. The 38th Division attacked a heavily fortified wooded area. German forces were well equipped with machine guns and the Welsh Division had to cross an exposed area of ground and suffered heavy losses before finally taking the Wood after vicious "hand to hand" fighting.

The Welsh Memorial at Mametz Wood

Author's own photograph

15th Battalion Royal Welsh Fusiliers

The 15th Battalion Royal Welsh Fusiliers was raised on the 20th October 1914. In December 1914 they joined 128th Brigade, 43rd Division, at Llandudno, which was then renamed the 113th Brigade 38th Welsh Division on the 28th April 1915. They moved to Winchester for final training in August 1915 and proceeded to France in December 1915.

In July 1916 the Battalion saw action at Mametz Wood on the Somme, suffering severe casualties.

The Division did not return to the Front Line for more than 12 months. In 1917 the Battalion saw action in the Third Battle of Ypres.

In 1918 the Army was reorganised and on 27th February 1918, the 15th Battalion Royal Welsh Fusiliers was disbanded and troops transferred to other units.

The 15th Battalion Royal Welsh Fusiliers on Parade in Llandudno in 1915

Hedd Wyn (13 January 1887 – 31 July 1917)

Hedd Wyn was born Ellis Humphrey Evans, on the 13th of January 1887 at Penlan, a house in the centre of Trawsfynydd, Merionethshire. Ellis enlisted in February 1917 and received his training at Litherland Camp, Liverpool, but in March 1917, the Government called for former farm workers, in the Military, to help with the ploughing and general farming. Ellis was temporarily released to work on his family's farm. During that time, Ellis submitted his poetry to the National Eisteddofod.

In June 1917, he joined the 15th Battalion Royal Welsh Fusiliers (part of the 38th Division).

Ellis was killed on the 31st of July 1917, during the Battle of Pilkham Ridge, Battle of Passchendale, known as the Third Battle of Ypres.

He was posthumously awarded the "Black Chair" for his poem "Hero," that he entered into the National Eisteddfod and was given his Bardic name Hedd Wyn, meaning "Blessed Peace"

The greatest honour for any Welsh poet is to win the chair at the National Eisteddfod.

One of his poems-

"War (Rhyfel)"

Woe that I live in bitter days
As God is setting like a sun
And in His place, as Lord and slave
Man raises forth his heinous throne

When he thought God was gone at last
He put his brother to the sword
Now death is roaring in our ears
Shadowing the shanties of the poor

The old and silenced harps are hung
On yonder willow trees again
The bawl of boys is on the wind
Their blood is blended in the rain

16th (Service) Battalion Royal Welsh Fusiliers

The 16th (Service) Battalion Royal Welsh Fusiliers was raised at Llandudno in November 1914 by the Welsh National Executive Committee from recruit's surplus to the 13th Battalion. Later in the month, they joined 128th Brigade 43rd Division at Llandudno, which was renamed 113th Brigade 38th (Welsh) Division on the 28th April 1915. The Battalion moved to Winchester for final training in August 1915 and proceeded to France in December 1915. In July 1916 they were in action at Mametz Wood on the Somme, suffering severe casualties, the Division did not return to major action for more than 12 months. In 1917 the Battalion were in action in the Third Battle of Ypres, then in 1918 they returned to action on the Somme In the Battles of the Hindenburg Line and the final advance in Picardy.

Demobilisation began in December 1918 and was completed by June 1919.

Photograph shows soldiers marching through Winchester from The Morn Hill Camp. This was one of the largest Military camps of the First World War and was a tempoary home for the 16th Battalion Royal Welsh Fusiliers and thousands of other soldiers. Approx 2 million soldiers passed through Winchester during World War I to board the train to take them to Sounthampton and onto France.

17th (2nd North Wales) Battalion Royal Welsh Fusilier

The 17th Battalion (2nd North Wales) Royal Welsh Fusiliers was raised at Llandudno on 2nd February 1915. They trained in Llandudno joining the 113th Brigade 38th Welsh Division on the 28th of April 1915. They moved to Winchester for final training in August 1915 and proceeded to France in December 1915. In July 1916 they took part in the infamous Battle of Mametz Wood on the Somme, suffering severe casualties. The 38th Division did not return to major action for more than 12 months. In 1917 the Battalion were in action in the Third Battle of Ypres, then in 1918 they returned to action on the Somme in the Battles of the Hindenburg Line and the final advance in Picardy. Demobilisation began in December 1918 and was completed by June 1919.

Officers of the 17th Battalion Royal Welsh Fusiliers 1915

> 'The wounded and dead around us, friends falling never to rise again'
>
> Sergeant John Charles Rowlands,
> 17th Royal Welsh Fusiliers

Quote by Sergeant John Charles Rowlands 17th Battalion Royal Welsh Fusiliers Whilst Fighting on the Western Front

H. M. A. S. A. E. 1
Australian Navy

His Majesty's Australian submarine A. E. 1 was launched in the yard of Vickers Ltd at Barrow in Furness, England on 22nd May 1913. She was commissioned at Portsmouth on the 28th February 1914 under the command of Lieutenant Commander Thomas Fleming Besant R.N, she was the first of two E Class Submarines built for the fledgling Royal Australian Navy and was manned by Royal Navy Officers with a mixed crew of saliors drawn from the Royal Navy and the Royal Australian Navy.

Accompanied by her Sister Submarine A. E. 2, under the command of Lieutenant Commander Henry Stoker R.N, A. E. 1 departed England in March 1914, although the Submarines remained surfaced for almost all of the delivery voyage, it was , at this time, the longest transit distance ever travelled by a Submarine.

At the outbreak of World War 1, A. E. 1 joined the Navel Forces assigned to the capture of the German Pacific Colonies with A. E. 2. She took part in the operations leading to the occupation of German New Guinea, including the surrender of Rabaul on the 13th September 1914.

The following day at 7.00am, the destroyer H. M. A. S. Parramatta left her night patrol ground,off Raluna Point and proceeded at a slow pace in the direction of Cape Gazelle to rendevous with A. E. 1 and conduct a patrol in St. Georges Channel to the South and east of the Duke of York Islands, the two vessels met off Herburtschute at 8.ooam and exchanged signals, before proceeding to Cape Gazelle, where they arrived at approximately 9.00am. A further exchange of signals followed during which Paramatta advised A. E. 1 that her orders were to search to the South' ard with Submarine and anchor off Herbertshone at 5.30am.

Parramatta proceeded independently in a Southern direction while A. E. 1 advanced in a North-easterly direction. The weather was hazy and visability was observed to be between 9 and 10 nautical miles at times decreasing to 5 miles. Parramatta reported that A. E. 1 was obscured by the haze for sometime, given the conditions, Parramatta's Commanding Officer, Lieutenant William Warren R A N, considered it advisable not to lose sight of the submarine for too long.

At 12.30 Parrmatta turned to the North-west and by 2.30pm, she was close to A. E. 1 when the Submarine asked by signal "What is the distance visability?" Parramatta responded "About 5 miles". At 3.20pm the Submarine was lost sight of and Parramatta altered course and steamed in the direction she was last seen. No sign of A. E. 1 was found and it was considered that she must have steamed back to the harbour without informing Parramatta. Consequently, Parramatta proceeded to the North-west and rounded Duke of York Island, before heading to Credner Island, later anchoring off Herburtshohe at 7.00pm.

By 8.00pm the Submarine had not returned and Parramatta and her Sister Ship H. M. A. S. Yarra were ordered to search for the Submarine. The light cruiser H. M. A. S. Sydney, also received instructions to keep a look-out, H. M. A. S Encounter and Warego also joined the search.

No traces of A. E. 1 was found, not even the tell-tale shimmer of escaping oil floating on the surface of the water.

The loss of A. E. 1 with her enitre complement of 3 Officers and 32 Sailors was the RAN's first major tragedy.

It is not known what caused A. E. 1 to sink without trace.

Many searches have taken place since 1976 to establish her location, none were successful.

In December 2017 a new search, using the vessle Furgo Equntor, located the wreck of A. E. 1 in 300 metres of water off the Duke of York island group.

In April 2018 an expedition was conducted to perform a detailed remotely operated vehicle (ROV) survey of the wreck of the A. E. 1, a team of experts are now analysing the footage to better understand what happened.

Last known image of AE1, 9 September 1914 with Yarra and Australia in the background.

April 2018 ROV Photograph of the Wreck of the A. E. 1

HMA Submarine *AE1*

Battle Honours: Rabaul 1914

In early September 1914, HMA Submarines AE1 and AE2 deployed with the Australian fleet to occupy Germany's regional possessions in the South-West Pacific and remove the threat posed by the German East Asiatic Cruiser Squadron. Following a successful operation to seize Rabaul, AE1 was conducting a patrol with the destroyer HMAS Parramatta in St George's Channel, to the south and east of Duke of York Island, when she vanished on the afternoon of 14 September 1914. Despite an extensive search conducted over a three-day period, no trace was found of the submarine or its 35 crew (14 Royal Australian Navy and 21 Royal Navy).

Entombed but not forgotten

Submarines Association of Australia

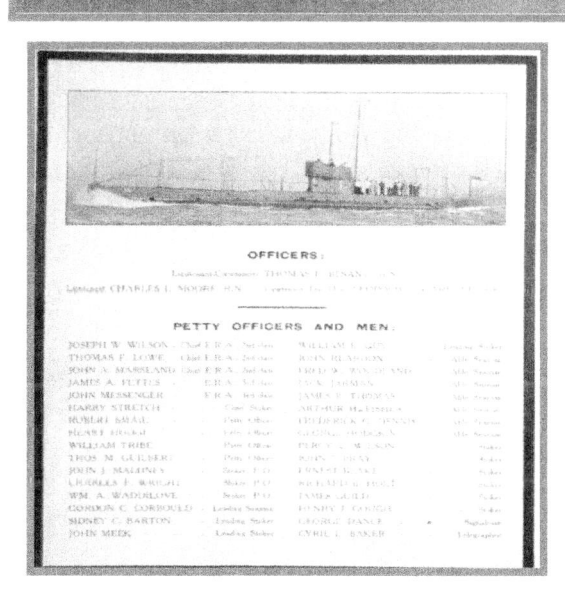

Memorial Plaques of the Submarine

The Royal Naval Reserve

The Royal Naval Reserve (RNR) on mobilisation in 1914, consisted of 30,000 Officers and men.

Officers of the permanent RNR or general service quickly took up seagoing appointments in the fleet, many in command of Destroyers, Submarines, Auxillary Cruisers and Q Ships. Others served in larger units of the battle fleet. Fishermen of the RNR section served with distinction on board trawlers fitted out as minesweepers, for mine clearance operations abroad and at home throughout the War, where they suffered heavy casualties and losses.

A number of the RNR Officers qualified as Pilots and flew Aircraft and Airships with the Royal Naval Air Service, whilst many RNR ratings served ashore alongside the RN and RNVR contingents in the trenches of the Somme and at Gallipoli with the Royal Naval Division.

Merchant Service Offiers and men serving in the Armed Merchant Cruisers, Hospital Ships, Fleet Auxillaries and Transports were enrolled in the RNR for the duration of the War on special agreements.

Although considerably smaller than both the RN and the RNVR, the RNR had an excellent War record, with 12 Victoria Crosses being awarded.

The 2nd Battalion Border Regiment

The 2nd Battalion Border Regiment was based at Pembroke Dock when War broke out in August 1914. On the 5th September they moved to Lyndhurst to join the 20th Brigade in the 7th Division. They landed at Zeebrugge on the 6th October 1914 and in 1915 were in action at the Battle of Neuve Chapelle, the Battle of Aubers, the Battle of Festubert, the Second Action of Givenchy and the Battle of Loos. In 1916, they moved to the Somme and were in action at Mametz, the Battle of Bazentin and the attacks on High Wood, the Battle of Delville Wood, the Battle of Guillemont and Operations on the Ancre. In 1917 they took part in the German retreat to the Hindenburg Line, the Arras Offensive in the Flanking Operations around Bullecourt, the Third Battle of Ypres including the Battle of Polygon Wood, the Battle of Broodseinde, the Battle of Poelcapelle and the Second Battle of Passchendale. At the end of 1917, the 7th Division were ordered to Italy and in October 1918, they had a central role in crossing the river Piave and were in action in the Battle of Vittoria Veneto.

The 4th Battalion South Wales Borderers

Formed at Brecon as part of the Kitchener's New Army in August 1914, they came under orders of the 40th Brigade 13th (Western) Division.

They moved to Park House Camp at Tidworth and in October 1914 went on to Chisledon and were in Billetts in Cirencester by December 1914,

The Battalion moved to Woking in March 1915 and embarked at Avonmouth on the 29th June 1915, sailing to Gallipoli via Mudros and landing on Gallipoli on the 15th July 1915.

They left Gallipoli for Mudros in Jnauary 1916 and saw action in Egypt and Mesopotamia.

The Brecon County Times – August 21st 1919

The welcome home parade having to be cancelled due to the outbreak of influenza and pnemonia on the ship home

The 12th (Service) Battalion Highland Light Infantry (City of Glasgow Regiment)

12th (Service) Battalion, Highland Light Infantry (City of Glasgow Regiment) was raised at Hamilton in September 1914 as part of Lord Kitchener's Second New Army and joined the 46th Brigade in the 15th Scottish Division. They moved to Bordon for training and in March 1915 moved to Romsey then to Chisledon Camp on Sailsbury Plain for final training in April 1915. They were in action in the Battle of Loos in 1915 and in Spring 1916, they were involved in the German Gas Attacks near Hulluch and the Defence of the Kink Position. They were in action during the Battle of the Somme including the Battle of Pozieres, the Battle of Flers-Courcelette and the capture of Martinpuich, the Battle of Le-Trtansloy and the attacks on the Butte De Warlencourt.

In 1917 they were in action in the First and Second Battle of Scarpe, including the capture of Guemappe during the Arras Offensive. On the 3rd of February 1918 they transferred to 106th Brigade 35th Division, they saw action in the Battle of Courtrai and Tieghem during the final advance in Flanders.

The 13th (Kensington) Battalion County of London Regiment

The 13th (Kensington) Battalion County of London Regiment were a unit of the Territorial Force with their Headquarters (HQ) at Iverna Gardens, Kensington. They were serving with the 4th London Brigade 2nd London Division when War broke out in August 1914. They were at once mobilised for War and moved to Abbotts Langley. They proceeded to France, landing at Le Harve on the 4th of November and joined the 25th Briagade 8th Division on the 13th of the same month. They saw action at the Battle of Neuve Chapelle and the Battle of Aubers. On the 20th of May 1915 they transferred to GHQ Troops and formed a composite unit with the 1/5th and 1/12th Londons. On the 11th February 1916 they transferred to 168th Brigade in the newly reformed 56th (London) Division in the Hallencourt Area. In 1916 they were in action on the 1st day of the Battle of the Somme, taking part in the diversionary attack at Gommecourt, the Battle of Ginchy, the Battle of Flers-Courcelette, the Battle of Morval and the Battle of Transloy Ridges. In 1917 they were in action at the Hindenburg Line and the Battle of Arras in April, The Battle of Langemarck in August, then the Cambrai Operations in November.

In 1918 they were in action on the Somme, the Second Battles of Arras, the Hindenburg Line and the Final Advance in Picardy. Demobilisation was completed on the 18th of May 1919.

The 3/5th Battalion King's Liverpool Regiment

Formed in Liverpool on 17th May 1915 were very quickly moved to Weeton Camp near Blackpool. On the 8th April 1916, became the 5th and 6th Reserve Battalions and on the 1st September 1916 the 6th was absorbed into the 5th.

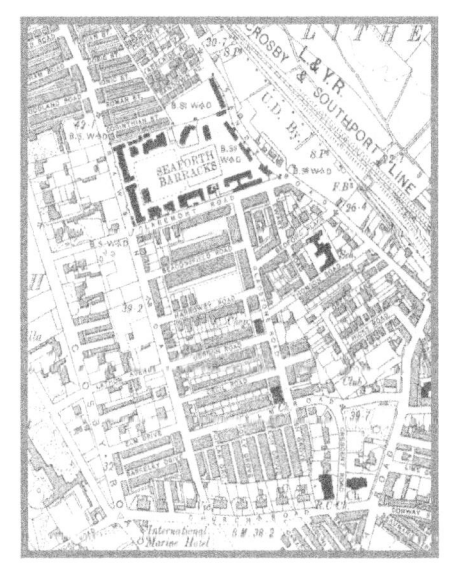

Seaforth Camp Liverpool in 1914. Located just off Crosby Road between the Seaforth and the Litherland areas of the City

Weeton Camp, Blackpool

The Pembroke Yeomanry (Castlemartin)

The Regiment was formed on the creation of the Territorial Force in April 1908 and placed under the orders of the South Wales Mounted Brigade. It was Headquartered at Tenby with the squadrons being placed as follows:

- A Squadron: Tenby (with Drill Stations at Pembroke, St. Florence, Manorbier, Kilgetty and Templeton)

- B Squadron: Haverfordwest (Clarbeston Road, Newgale and Fishguard)

- C Squadron: Carmarthen (Whitland, Llanelli, Llandilo, Llangadock, Pantglas and Llandovery)

- D Squadron: Lampeter (Aberystwyth, Tregaron, Llandyssil and Llandbyther

The 1st Pembroke (Castlemartin) Yeomanry

The 1st Pembroke (Castlemartin) Yeomanry in August 1914, moved to Hereford after mobilising, then to Thetford (Norfolk) and came under orders of 1st Mounted Division. In November 1915 dismounted. In March 1916 they moved to Egypt and on arrival the Brigade merged with the Welsh Border Mounted Brigade and formed the 4th Dismounted Brigade. On the 2nd February 1917, they merged with 1/1st Glamorgan Yeomanry to form the 24th Pembroke and Glamorgan Yeomanry Battalion. The Regiment came under orders of the 231st Brigade in the 74th Yeomanry Division and moved to France in 1918.

2/1st Pembroke Yeomanry

2/1st Pembroke Yeomanry was formed as a Second Line Regiment in September 1914 and moved to Camarthen in early 1915. Moved to Llandilo and by September of that year, were at Yoxford. In June 1916 they converted to a Cyclist Unit under the orders of 2nd Cyclist Brigade. In November 1916 the Regiments merged with 2/1st Glamorgan Yeomanry to form 2nd Pembroke and Glamorgan Yeomanry Cyclist Regiment. In March 1917 the Yeomanry was at Aldeburgh. They moved in July to Benacre and by the end of the year moved to Lowestoft, where it remained.

3/1st Pembroke Yeomanry

3/1st Pembroke Yeomanry formed as a Third Line Training Unit at Camarthen in May 1915 and then moved to Brecon. In the summer of 1916, they dismounted and attached to the 3rd Line Groups of the Welsh Division at Oswestry. In February 1917, they disbanded, with some men going to the 2/1st Pembroke Yeomanry and the others to the the 4th Reserve Battalion of the Welsh Regiment at Milford Haven.

78th Seige Battery Royal Garrison

78th Siege Battery Royal Garrison Artillary were equipped with heavy Howitzers, sending large calibre high explosive shells in high trajectory.

The usual armaments were 6", 8" and 9.2" Howitzers.

The Seige Batteries were most often employed in destroying or neutralising the enemy artillery, as well as putting destructive fire down on strong points, store dumps, road and railways, behind enemy lines.

The 78th Siege Battery arrived in France on the 15th April 1916.

The 78th Siege Battery, from April 1916, had four 8" Howitzers, this was increased to six, by 1918.

The 8" Howitzer Mark VI, VII, and VIII were a series of artillery single Howitzers. They were designed by Vickers in Britain and produced by all four British artillery manufactures but mainly by Armstrong. They delivered a 200lb bagged charge shell, up to a distance of 12, 300 yards.

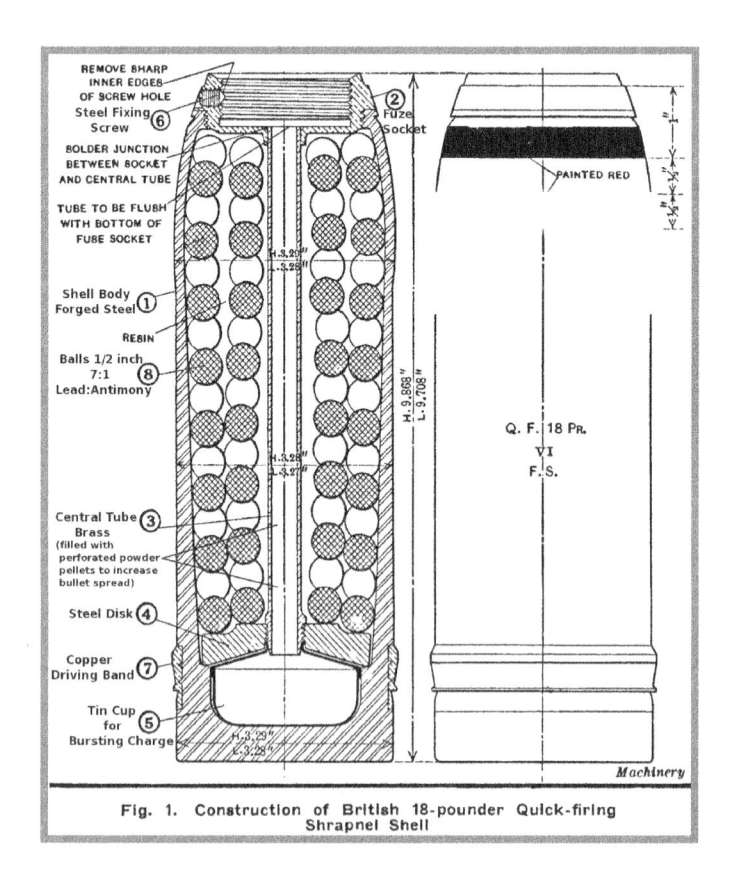

Fig. 1. Construction of British 18-pounder Quick-firing Shrapnel Shell

Royal Defence Corps

The Royal Defence Corps was formed in 1916 by the conversion of the Garrison Battalions of the Infantry Regiments on the Home Service, which were made up of conscripts and soldiers either too old or medically unfit for service overseas. The Protection Companies of the RDC provided troops to guard the infastructure of the UK, such as, Ports, Bridges andF, and also to guard Military and Prisoner of War Camps, taking over duties from the Territorial Units.

The Observing Companies took over the duties of keeping watch over the coast and skies for enemy activity.

R. A. M. C. Royal Army Medical Corps

The Royal Army Medical Corps was formed on the 23rd June 1898. The R. A. M. C. that took to the field in France in 1914 was a vastly different service by 1918.

At the outbreak of the Great War there were 9,000 Warrant Officers and men of the R. A. M. C., this grew to 113,000 by 1918.

It was quickly realised that a man's chances of survival depended on how quickly his wound was treated. The War was now producing vast numbers of casulalties requiring treatment at the same time, it was impossible for Surgeons to evaluate and treat the wounded successfully on the Front Line, that is why a chain of evacuation was set up.

The R. A. M. C. was not a fighting force but it's members saw the full horror of the War, the Warrant Officers and men preformed their duties unarmed, the R. A. M. C. lost no less than 6,873 personnel during the conflict, of these, were either killed in action or died of their wounds.

3, 002 Military Medals

395 Distinguished Conduct Medals

1,484 Military Crosses

499 Distinguised Service Orders

7 Victoria Crosses

These were awarded to the members of the R. A. M. C. during the Great War.

The Royal Army Medical Corps by F. Matania: Welcome Collection

A Group of R. A. M. C. Men

Chapter 5
Evacuation Of The Wounded

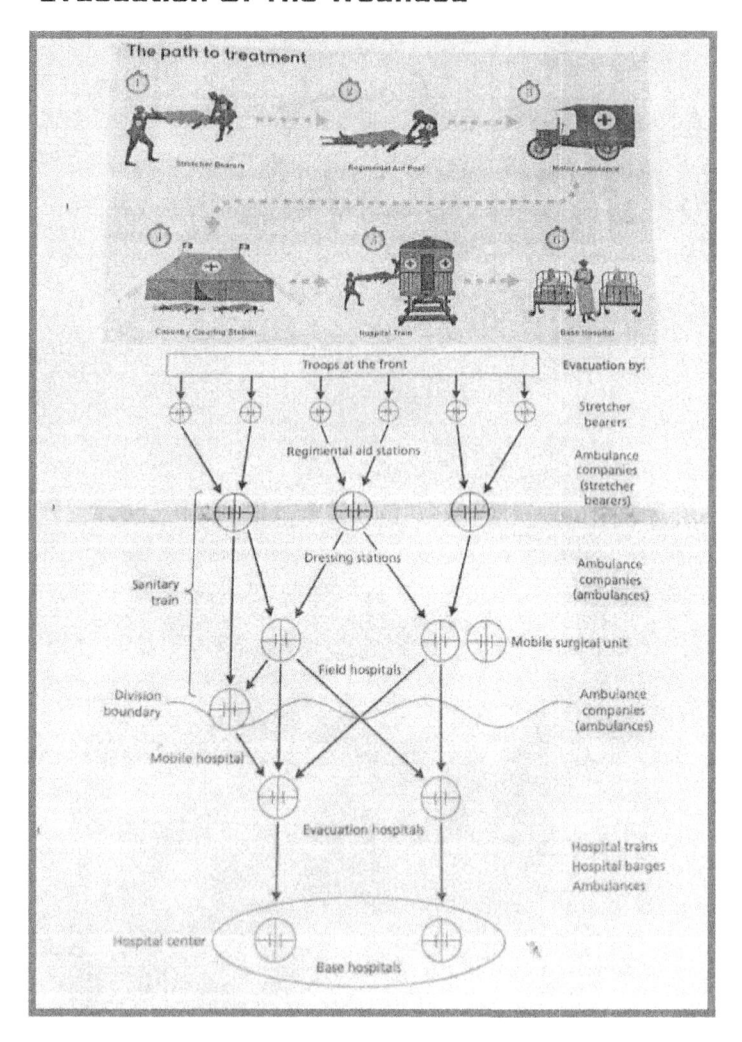

The Chain of Evacuation was one of the most important and effective systems set up so wounded soldiers could be treated in a safe area. There were 4 main stages. The order may not have been the same for all casualties

Regimental Aid Stations

The casualty is likely to have received first medical attention at an Aid Post, situated close behind the front line position. Units in the trenches generally had a Medical Officer, Orderlies and Stretcher Bearers who would provide support. These positions were well within range of enemy fire.

Advance Dressing Station

There was no set rule regarding the location of the Advanced Dressing Station. Existing buildings, underground bunkers and dugouts, were the most common because they gave some protection from enemy shellfire. The dressing stations were manned by R. A. M. C. Royal Army Medical Corps. In times of heavy fighting, the Advance Dressing Stations would be overwhelmed by the volume of casualties and often wounded men had to lie in the open on stretchers, until they were seen to.

Field Ambulance

This was a Mobile Medical Unit.

Each British Division had 3 such units as well as a Specialist Medical Sanitary Unit.

As well as serving the Aid and Bearer Post, they also established Main and Advanced Dressing Stations, where a casualty, could receive further treatment and could be prepared for evacuation to a Casualty Clearing Station.

Casualty Clearing Station (C.C.S.)

Once treated at the Dressing Station, casualties would be moved several miles to the rear, this might be on foot, horse-drawn wagon or motorised ambulance or lorry, or in some cases by light railway.

The C. C. S. was the first large, well-equipped and static medical facility that the wounded men would visit. It's role was to retain all serious cases that were unfit for further travel. They hoped to treat and return injured cases to their units. All others would be treated, then evacuated to a Base Hospital. It was often a tented camp, although, where possible, wooden huts were used

The C. C. S. were usually a few miles behind the lines close to a railway line.

A typical C. C. S. would house up to 1,000 casualties at any given time. At peak times of battle, even the C.C. S. struggled with the influx of casualties.

Serious operations, such as limb amputations were carried out here. They also treated nervous disorders and infectious diseases.

The transport infastructure of the railways usually dictated their location, once the casualty was ready to be moved to a Base Hospital or directly to a Port for embarkation (known as a Blighty Wound), this was always by rail.

There were 4 ambulance trains in 1914 and 28 by July 1916 on the Western Front.

The serious nature of many wounds defied the mediacl facilities and skills of the C. C. S. and many C. C. S. positions are today marked by large Military Cemetries.

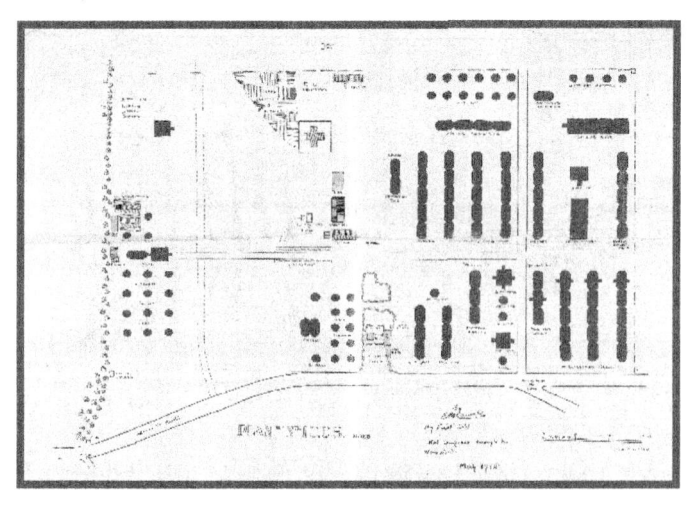

No. 1 Casualty Clearing Station Plan

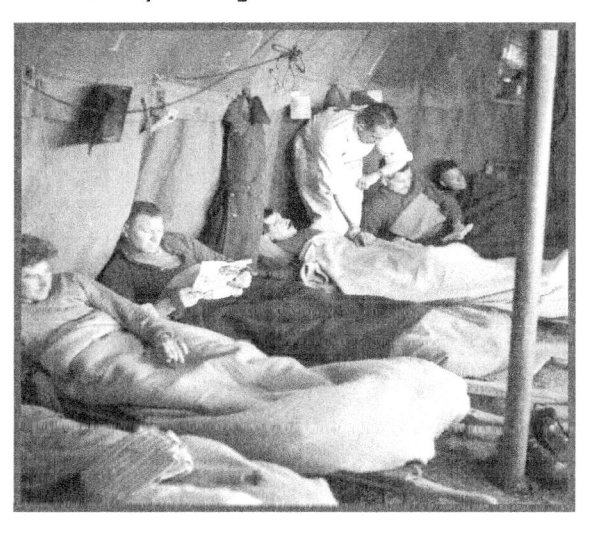

Hospital Ambulance Train

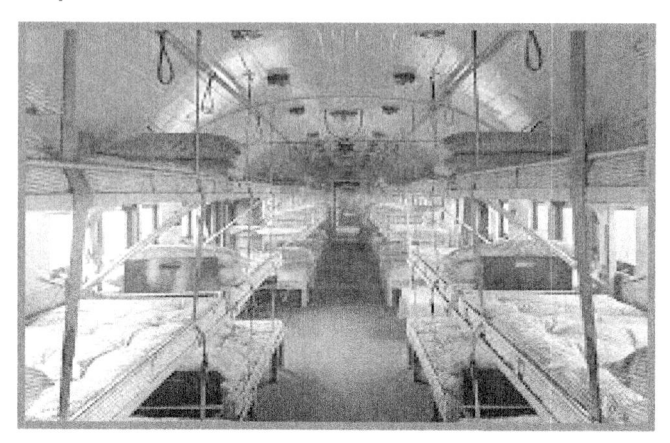

These trains transported the wounded from the C. C. S. to Base Hospitals near one of the channel ports.

Base Hospital

Once admitted to a Base Hospital the casualty stood a reasonable chance of survival. Half of the occupants of a Base Hospital were sent for further treatment or convalescence in the UK.

Home Hospital

Existing Military Hospitals in the UK were expanded. Many Civilian Hospitals were turned over in full or part to Military use.

Chapter 6
The Missing

When a soldier was declared as "missing", his next of kin would be informed.

They would then endure a period of months whilst enquiries were made to find details of their loved ones, sometimes via neutral agencies, to see if the enemy had information as to their death or capture. If no information was forthcoming, a formal presumption of a man's death was made, but what happened to his Army pay in the meantime? It was a vital matter for many families, already struggling to cope without their Husband, Father, Son, etc.

Army council instruction 17 of 1916 made it all clear: -

"The general rule is that pay should be credited up to the actual date of death, where this is not defintiely ascertained, but where that date is not known, pay can only be credited to a date four weeks after that on which the next of kin was notified that the soldier was missing.

If evidence of an actual date of death was forthcoming, any pay that had been credited beyond that date, would be re-credited to the public purse."

(In other words, if they pay you too much, you have to pay it back!)

My Boy Jack by Rudyard Kipling

Have you the news of my boy Jack?
Not this tide
When d'you think that he'll come back?
Not with this wind blowing and this tide

Has anyone else had word of him?
Not this tide
For what is sunk will hardly swim
Not with this wind blowing and this tide

Oh dear, what comfort can I find?
None this tide
Nor any tide
Except he did not shame his kind –
Not even with that wind blowing, and that tide

Then hold your head up all the more
This tide
And every tide
Because he was the Son you boreAnd gave to that wind blowing and that tide

Rudyard Kipling's son Jack was killed on the Western Front in September 1915 at the Battle of Loos. Jack had only been in France for three weeks and because of his very poor eyesight had initally been rejected by the Army. Only through the intervention of his famous Father, that he was accepted for a commission in the Irish Guards. Jack was reported missing and his body was never found until many years later

Rudyard Kipling & his Son Jack

Chapter 7
Burying The Fallen in WW1

The Imperial War Graves Commission (I. W. G. C.) was the British institution that dealt with burying and commemorating First World War dead and missing soldiers.

Today it is known as the Commonwealth War Graves Commission C. W. G. C. (name changed in 1960 to reflect the changing state of the British Empire) and is responsible for Cemetries and Memorials of both World Wars In more than 150 countries. Partly in response to his Son Jack's death, Rudyard Kipling joined Sir Fabian Ware's Imperial War Graves Commission. This group was responsible for the beautiful War Graves that can be found all over the Western Front and beyond. Kipling is responsible for the Biblical phrase "Their Name Liveth Forever More", found on the stones of remberence in the larger War Cemetries and for the phrase "Known Unto God" for the Gravestones of the unidentified servicemen. He also chose the phrase "The Glorious Dead" on the Cenotaph Whitehall London.

Families were allowed to choose 66 words epitaphs for headstones. Initially, they were charged 3 ½ D per letter, but the commission soon faced accusations of hypocrisy, because only the wealthy could afford a substantial inscription.

Tyne Cot Cemetery Belgium

The two phrases of Rudyard Kipling

Chapter 8
The Home Front

On the Home Front, families were encouraged to send letters, food parcels, socks, cigarettes and tobacco, to keep up the spirits of the men fighting at the front. Parcels were delivered very quickly to the soldiers on the Front Line.

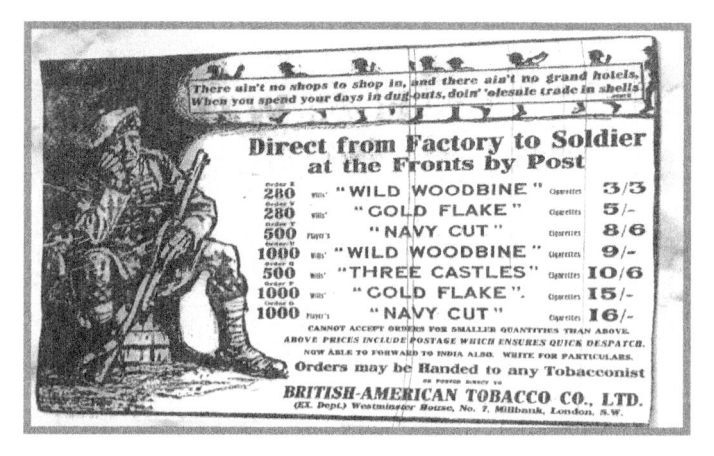

Advertisment appeared in the County Herald 2nd November 1916

Advert for items to be sent to Officers on the Front Line

Reporting the News

It was important that the local Newspapers reported the War to the families back at home. Here are a few examples of some of the articles that appeared in the County Herald and the Flintshire Observer during this time.

Correspondance From the Front

The soldiers on the Front Line would write letters and postcards back home to their loved ones. All letters and postcards were censored by the soldiers Commanding Officers to make sure no information was given on the Battalions location, that could then fall into enemy hands. Here are a few examples of the postcards sent home.

Chapter 9
Coming Home

Coming home from the War could be defined in two ways: -

Coming home wounded, or coming home when the War was over

Two very different scenarios.

Wounded

When coming home wounded, the level of treatment depended on the severity of the injuries, whether physical or mental.

The Red Cross

Following the outbreak of the War, in August 1914, The British Red Cross formed the Joint War Commitee with the Order of St. John (known today as St. John's Ambulance). They fund raised and worked together under the protective emblem of The Red Cross. The Joint War Committee organised volunteers and professional staff, it also supplied machinery and services, at home, and in the conflict areas of Europe, the Middle East and East Africa.

Working Parties

Red Cross working parties organised the supply of clothing for soldiers in hospitals, they also made vital hospital items such as bandages, splints, swabs and clothing.

Voluntary Aid Detatchments (VADs)

Members of the British Red Cross and the Order of St. John were organised into Voluntary Aid Detachments (V.A.D.s). The term VAD was used for an individual member as well as a detachment. All members were trained in first aid and some trained in nursing, cookery, hygiene and sanitation. The majority of female VADs volunteered as nurses, trained by the Red Cross, they were despatched throughout the UK and Europe during the conflict.

Rest Stations

At train stations, VADs provided food and supplies, such as cigarettes, to soldiers arriving by ambulance train.

Missing and Wounded Service

In 1915 the London branch of the Red Cross appointed VAD members to make enquiries at London hospitals, because families did not know where their loved ones were. The VADs were provided with lists of missing Officers and men and reported to the Red Cross Headquarters. Later this was expanded and taken over by the Red Cross Headquarters. There were offices in the UK, Paris, Boulogne, Rouen, Malta, Alexandria and Salonika. These looked for missing soldiers in hospitals. By the end of the First World War, the Red Cross had provided 90,000 VADs at home and abroad.

Auxiliary Hospitals

The Red Cross provided Auxiliary Hospitals and Convalescent Homes for wounded servicemen. Many people offered their properties to help. Hospitals were set up in Town Halls, Schools and Private Houses.

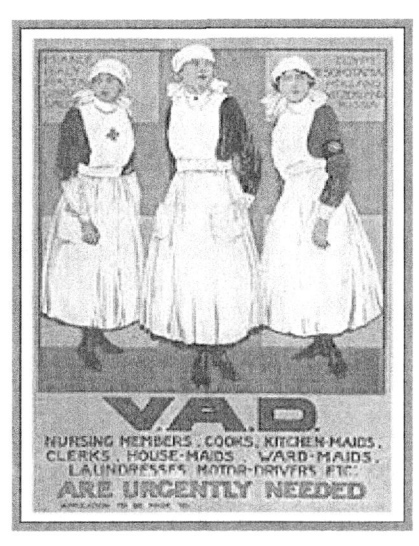

Recruiting Posters for the Red Cross

This is a VAD service card for Elizabeth Ayer, Mother of Leonard Stuart Ayer who is named on the Holywell Memorial

Photographs of the VADs at Holywell Drill Hall

Lluesty Hospital During the Great War

During the First World War, under the instructions of the Government, Lluesty was partly converted into a Military Hospital. On the 17th August 1917, patients started to arrive and by January 1918, there were 20 extra beds for wounded soildiers and no less than 477 military patients were treated up to the end of the War. The last group of soldiers were discharged on 30th January 1919. In 1925, there still remained at Lluesty, several former soldiers, regarded as "quarrelsome", perhaps this is another word for "shell shock?"

Pentreffynon Convalescent Home

This Convalescent Home was organised by Lady Mary Mostyn, with the help of St. Johns and had a facility of 16 beds, taking in only the "rank and file".

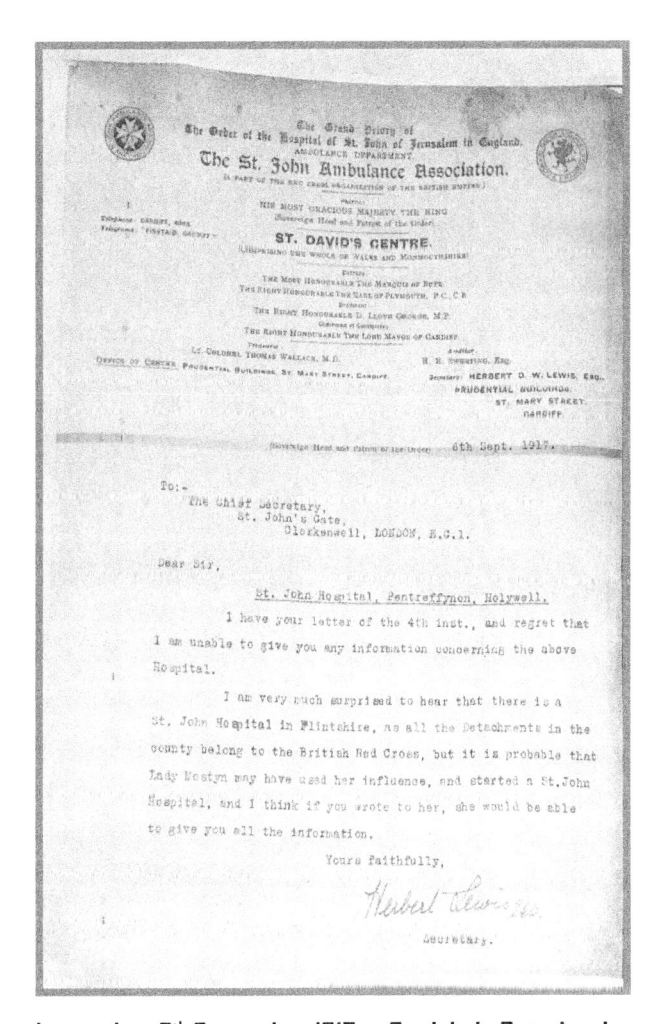

The Grand Priory of
The Order of the Hospital of St. John of Jerusalem in England.
AMBULANCE DEPARTMENT

The St. John Ambulance Association.
(AS PART OF THE RED CROSS ORGANISATION OF THE BRITISH EMPIRE.)

Patron:
HIS MOST GRACIOUS MAJESTY THE KING
(Sovereign Head and Patron of the Order.)

ST. DAVID'S CENTRE.
(COMPRISING THE WHOLE OF WALES AND MONMOUTHSHIRE)

Patrons:
THE MOST HONOURABLE THE MARQUIS OF BUTE
THE RIGHT HONOURABLE THE EARL OF PLYMOUTH, P.C., C.B.

Professor:
THE RIGHT HONOURABLE D. LLOYD GEORGE, M.P.
(Chairman of Committee)
THE RIGHT HONOURABLE THE LORD MAYOR OF CARDIFF.

Treasurer:
LT.-COLONEL THOMAS WALLACE, M.D.

Auditor:
H. H. SWEETING, Esq.

Secretary: HERBERT D. W. LEWIS, ESQ.
PRUDENTIAL BUILDINGS,
ST. MARY STREET,
CARDIFF.

OFFICE OF CENTRE: PRUDENTIAL BUILDINGS, ST. MARY STREET, CARDIFF.

Sovereign Head and Patron of the Order. 6th Sept. 1917.

To:-
The Chief Secretary,
St. John's Gate,
Clerkenwell, LONDON, E.C.1.

Dear Sir,

St. John Hospital, Pentreffynon, Holywell.

I have your letter of the 4th inst., and regret that I am unable to give you any information concerning the above Hospital.

I am very much surprised to hear that there is a St. John Hospital in Flintshire, as all the Detachments in the county belong to the British Red Cross, but it is probable that Lady Mostyn may have used her influence, and started a St. John Hospital, and I think if you wrote to her, she would be able to give you all the information.

Yours faithfully,

Herbert Lewis
Secretary.

Letter date 6th September 1917 to St, John's Gate, London asking for details on the Convalescent Home in Flintshire

Coming Home – War is Over

It was a different story for the men that served during the conflict and came home "unscathed." These men were expected to return home and carry on with normal life, return to their families and jobs that they held previously, but life had changed.

The end of War time production along with increased labour supply from returning troops helped contribute to high unemployment and the decline in wages. Factories that produced War related items, live ammunition, shells, uniforms etc., were no longer needed. The Government had spent millions on the War and had run up a large national debt.

No job, no money; not the "land fit for hero's" as the soldiers were promised.

Many returning would have been suffereing from post traumatic stress disorder (PTSD), but this was unheard of in 1918/1919 and men were expected to just "Get On With It." Homecoming parades were held in Holywell and all servicemen who had served received a scroll from H. M. Lieutenant for the County of Flint, Hawarden Castle, 19th July 1919, thanking them for their service.

Town Hall Holywell – Official Party Welcoming the Soldiers Home

The Welcome Home Parade for the Soldiers through Holywell High Street

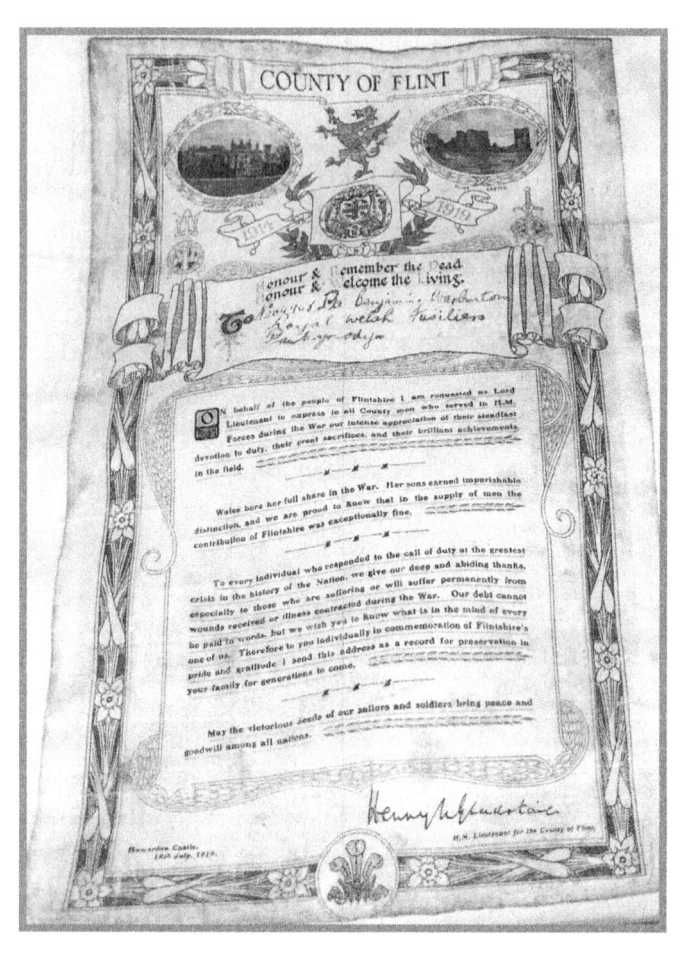

A Scroll Awarded to all Servicemen who Served in The First World War. Sent by the H. M. Lieutenant for the County of Flint.

The Scroll above is the Author's Great Uncle's

Chapter 10
My Taid (Grandfather)

My Taid, Edwin Roberts was born on 23rd June 1879 in Bootle, Liverpool. He married Mary Ellen Parry on the 4th June 1905 at Bethel Chapel, Pen-y-Ball Street, Holywell. His occupation at the time was a "Coal Cutter" and he lived at Hope Street Cottages, Bagillt. At the time of his enlistment in the Army, he was living at 17 Primrose Hill, Holywell. He joined the 10th (Service) Battalion Royal Welsh Fusiliers as a Private. His service number was 15736

The Battalion arrived in France on 27th September 1915. After moving up from the Port to Flanders, the Battalion arrived at the town of Bailleul on the 4th of October. From there, it moved to the Piggeries, a relatively safe location West of Ploegsteert Wood.

Over the next few days, the Battalion was taken in detachments to the Front Line on the far (Eastern) side of the wood, for familiarisation purposes, under the tutelage of another unit. It then withdrew back to Bailleul on the 9th October. The next day the 76th Brigade (including the Battalion) transferred to the command of the experienced regular 3rd Division.

The 10th Battalion Royal Welsh Fusiliers then moved forward towards the Ypres front, the War Diary mentions the arrival at a Belgian farm on the 10th October and gives a map reference of 28G18B. This makes the location "Line Farm", which is South of the hamlet of Brandhoek, halfway between Poperinge and Ypres (and is still there today).

On the 15th October the Battalion finally moved forward to relieve the 2nd Royal Scots who had been holding a sector of the Ypres front. The War Diary refers to A1 to A4, this was the area directly East of Ypres, North of the Menin Road and in the vicinity of the village of Hooge and Bellewarrde Farm. The British position ran through Railway Wood and the Y-Shaped Wood below.

Author Retracing his Taid's footsteps in Railway Wood August 29th 2016

Taid was wounded on the 18th October and suffered shrapnel wounds to his shoulder, chest and forearm. Taid's movements after this are very difficult to find, he would have been evacutated for hospital treatment.

Copy of the War Diary Showing the Reporting of my Taid's Wounding

I vaguely remember him saying that he returned to his Battalion and fought at Arras. His Army records show he was discharged from service on the 18th February 1919, under King's Regulations 392 XVIA.

His pension record states he also suffered gun shot wounds to the left hand and suffered from rheumatoid arthritis.

My Taid's Pension Record 30th June 1925

My Taid's Medal Index Card

My Taid had many jobs during his life time from being a Miner, to Council Worker. He worked hard all of his life and lost a Son (my Uncle) Elias in the Second World War.

Elias is also on a Holywell Memorial in Panton Place.

Elias (my Taid's Son) shown here in the middle of the photograph in Burma. Elias died in a Japanese Prisoner of War Camp 27th August 1943

The last years of Taid's life, after his Wife Mary, died in 1954, were spent with my Mam and Dad at our house in Coronation Estate (now known as Pen-y-Maes Gardens).

I always remember he called everyone "Joe" because he couldn't remember names. He always wore a shirt and tie and trilby and insisted on having a bath in the front room, in a tin bath, in front of the coal fire, even though we had a bathroom upstairs!

He used to walk down to the school gates to give sweets to my Sister Linda.

He was a tough old man. One time he fell and had stitches in his head, next day he had pulled them out because he said he didn't want them!

The last time I saw him alive was when he was in the old Cottage Hospital in Holywell. He had pneumonia. I called after school on the way home and asked to see my Taid. I always remember the Nurse asking me what his name was, I didn't know, I only knew his as Taid! Luckily, he must have heard me and shouted to the Nurse. He gave me some pennies for sweets, that was the last time I saw him.

I wish I could go back in time and ask him all the questions I have for him now.

I am proud of my Taid, for the service he and so many others have given to this Country.

Chapter 11
Dig Hill 80

Having had a keen interest in the First World War for many years, in 2018, myself, my partner Karen and her Mum, Julie, had the opportunity to join this great project.

Belgium Archeologist Simon Verdegem, along with Professor Peter Doyle and German Historian Robin Schafer, succeeded, through crowd funding, in raising the required budget to carry out an archelogical dig at the site. They gave the general public, like myself, Karen, my partner and Julie, her Mum, a chance to pay to have an opportunity to be part of this historic project.

Karen and Julie both have a keen interst in archelogy too and all of us were able to have a full day on the dig in Wijtschate in May 2018.

We decided to stay near Wijtschate for the weekend. On the day of the dig, we had a fantastic day digging the trenches. We were amongst approximately 30 like-minded volunteers; a day that we would never forget.

Simon and his team were incredible, we were treated, not as novices, but like an extension of his team.

Within an hour of digging the trenches I hit metal with my pick, Julie continued to carefully excavate around the metal and found it to be a rifle. Myself, Karen and Julie continued to dig and then Karen found, what she thought, was a piece of bone. We immediately called the experts over and after further examination, it was agreed that it was part of a jaw bone. We were moved to another part of the site, so the experts could carefully continue the recovery of the body, We later were told that there two bodies found, possibly two soldiers next to each other in the trench.

We continued, for the rest of the day, finding many things including bullets, buttons, communication cable and the trench ductboards.

What a fantastic day we had! something that will live with us for the rest of our lives.

In total, 110 bodies were recovered from the Dig Hill 80 site between April to July, mostly German soldiers, but 13 British and Commonwealth were also recovered.

We attended The Findings Presnataion in London, in 2018, with Al Murray, as host

The following year 2019, we returned to Belgium to attend the burial of the soldiers found at the site, a very moving ceremony indeed.

Dig Hill 80 Wijtschate Site

Nathan Howarth, Karen Humphreys,
Julie Humphreys & Simon Verdegem

Ben Casey, Julie Humphreys, Karen Humphreys & Russ Warburton
excavating the trench

Julie Humphreys excavating the trench

Russ Warburton with the completed excavation of the trench

Karen Humphreys gently clearing out the trench to reveal the ductboards

Nathan Howarth holding the rifle excavated from the first trench we were working on

Aerial view of the trenches at Dig Hill 80, Wijtschate

The villages and hills around Ypres in Belgium, saw some of the fiercest fighting in this region, in World War 1.

Wijtschate (British troops called it Whitesheet) or Dig Hill 80 as we know it, was one of them. After preliminary excavations on the largely German held stronghold by leading Belgian Archeologist Simon Verdegem, he was convinced that this area of land contained so many artifacts and more importantly, soldiers "missing" since the end of the Great War, time was of the essence as the land was set for property development.

Wijtschate is near Ypres, a Medieval Fort City in Flanders, just inland from Belgium's Northern coast. Ypres was crucial to Britain, both to halt Germany's charge towards Paris but to secure the Northern Channel Ports, that would allow it to safely ship soldiers to the continent. This is where advancing Germany sought access to the surrounding high ground. Hill 80 (or Hohe 80, to the Germans) was called this, because of its altitude, some 78.5 metres above sea level. This may not sound much, but in Flanders flat fields, from Hill 80, observations and artillary had a clear view of Ypres some 5 miles away. Within months of the conflict, the village of Wijtschate was all but flattened by artillary fire, but the subterranian trenches has a better chance of surviving the blast. Bavarian soldiers had also incorporated their trench network to criss-cross the cellars of existing buildings. The cellars could still be used long after the upper levels had collapsed.

Wijtschate at the end of the Battle in 1917

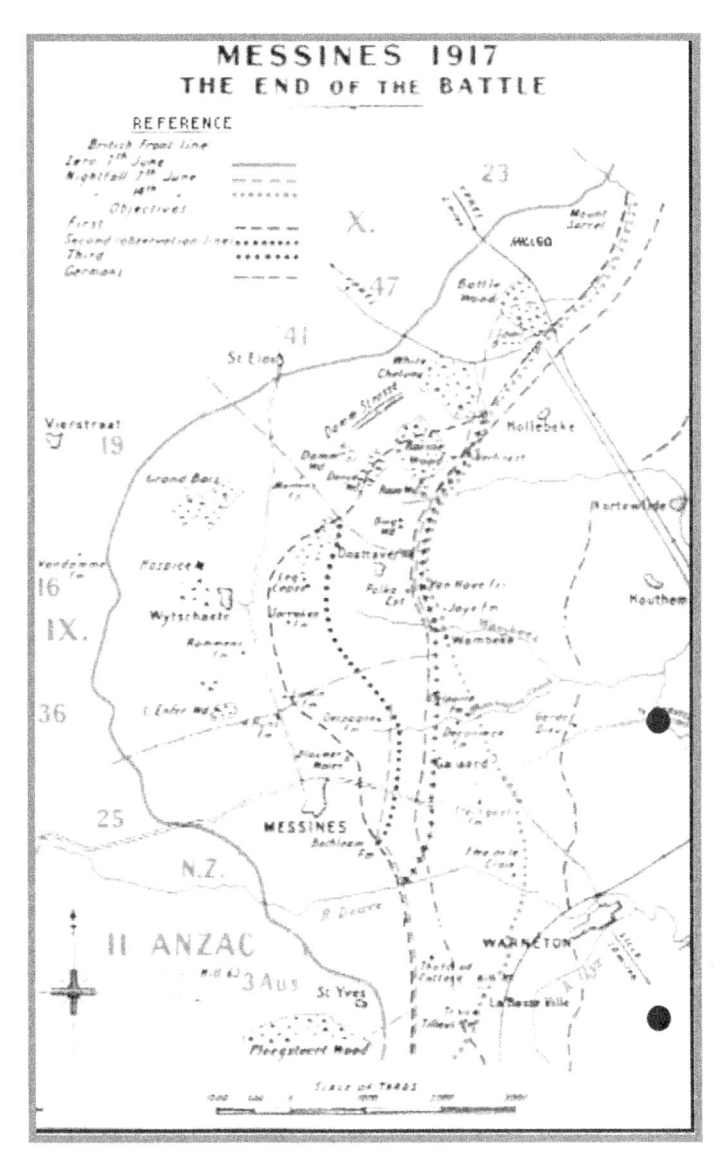

The Battle of Messines 1917

Chapter 12

List Of The Men Who Served from Holywell

1914 Star

Also known as the Mons Star, the medal is a bronze star with red, white and blue ribbon reflecting the French Tricolore.

It was issued to British Forces who had served in France or Belgium from 5th August 1914 (The Declaration of War), to Midnight 22nd November 1914 (End of First Battle of Ypres).

These were soldiers of the War that were there at the very beginning, and so, it was a primarily awarded to the "Old Contemptibles", the professional pre-war soldiers of the British Expeditionary Force (B. E. F.)

The recipients service number, rank, name and unit were impressed on the back.

1914-1915 Star

This bronze medal is very similar to the 1914 Star but has the dates 1914-1915 in the centre of the star. It was issued to much wider range of recipients, these included all who served in any theatre of War, outside the UK, between 5th August 1914 and 31st December 1915, except thoes eligible for the 1914 Star.

The recipients service number, rank, name and unit were impressed on the reverse.

British War Medal 1914-1920

The silver medal was awarded to Officers and men of the British and Imperial Forces who either entered a theatre of War (an area of acute fighting) or served overseas (perhaps a Garrison soldier) between 5th August and 11th November 1918.

This was later extended to services in Russia, Siberia and some other areas in 1919 and 1920.

The recipients service number, rank, name and unit were inscribed on the rim of the medal.

Victory Medal

The Allies each issued their own bronze Victory Medal, but with similar designs, equivalent wording and identical ribbon.

The colours of the ribbon represent the combined colours of Allied Nations, with the rainbow additionally representing the calm after the storm. The ribbon consists of a double rainbow with red at the centre

The British version depicts the winged figure of victory on the front of the medal and on the back it says "The Great War For Civilisation 1914-1919".

To qualify, an individual had to have entered a theatre of War (an area of active fighting), not just served overseas.

Their service number, rank, name and unit were impressed on the rim.

When the servicemen had returned home after the War had ended, they were asked to complete a card/form showing their record of service. These were then returned to Henry N. Gladstone Esq. H. M. Lieutenant for the County of Flint and are now kept at Hawarden Records Office. Each card was numbered and proceeded by a letter.

L = Living

F – Fallen

Also, if the person was deceased or missing, the right hand corner of the card is removed.

This is an example of the cards kept at Hawarden Record Office. This is a copy of my Taid's card Edwin Roberts.

The soldiers are listed as per the **L** number and all records are are available to view at Hawarden Records Office.

CARD NO.	NAME	ADDRESS
L1	WILLIAM JOHN AMES	10 BAGILLT STREET
F1	HERBERT EDWARD ABBOTT	2 SUMMERHILL
F3	LEONARD STUART AYER	THE COTTAGE, STRAND
L2	GEORGE BAILY	CHURCH HOUSE
L3	JAMES GILBERT BEATON	IVY HOUSE HIGH STREET
L4	RICHARD BEEDLES	25 GREENFIELD STREET
L4BRY	EDWARD BRACE	PWLL-MERYN FARM
L6	SYDNEY BICKERTON	1 PRIMROSE HILL
L7	ROBERT BOYES	DAVIES SQUARE, NEW ROAD
L8	STEPHEN BOYES	DAVIES SQUARE, NEW ROAD
L9	JOHN BOYLE	5 ALLAN SQUARE
L10	WILLIAM THOMAS BOYLE	5 ALLAN SQUARE
L10	EDWARD BEEDLES	4 BANK PLACE
L11	ANTHONY BOYLE	WHITFORD STREET
L12	LEONARD BRUNTON	19 WELL STREET
L13	JOSEPH BYWATER	CASTLE VIEW
F4	JOHN BOYES	DAVIES SQUARE, NEW ROAD
L15	THOMAS WILLIAM CARNEY	WELL STREET
L16	EDWIN JOHN CATHERWOOD	THE OBSERVER SHOP, HIGH STREET
L17	CHARLES S. CATHERWOOD	8 HIGH STREET
L18	RAPHAEL CATHERWOOD	8 HIGH STREET
L19	WALTER F. CATHERWOOD	8 HIGH STREET
L20	WILLIAM CATHERWOOD	8 HIGH STREET
L21	WILLIAM CHAMBERLAIN	THE HARP
L22	GEORGE CLARIDGE	VICTORIA
L23	FRANK CONLON	16 PRIMROSE HILL
L24	R. CONLON	16 PRIMROSE HILL
L25	ANTHONY CONLON	16 PRIMROSE HILL
F5	JOHN JAMES CONLON	16 PRIMROSE HILL
L27	WALTER LEONARD DAVIES	WHITFORD STREET

L28	THOMAS EDWARD DAVIES	39 WELL STREET
L29	THOMAS RALPH DAVIES	SCHOOL HOUSE, BRYNFORD STREET
L30	JOHN DAVIES	2 RED HOUSES
L31	SAMUEL GLADSTONE DAVIES	SUMMERHILL
L33	WILLIAM DEMPSEY	5 LOWER PRIMROSE HILL
L34	RICHARD DICKINSON	3 PANTON PLACE
L35	JOHN HERBERT DYKINS	PENDRE WHITFORD STREET
L36	JAMES DYKINS	TOWER GARDENS PLACE
L37	JAMES DYKINS	1 TOWER GARDENS
L7BRY	RICHARD DAVIES	LILY TERRACE, BRYNFORD
L10BRY	THOMAS GROSVENOR DAVIES	PEN-YR-HWYLFA
F6	JOHN EDWARD DAVIES	6 DOLPHIN COTTAGES
F7	ROBERT THOMAS DAVIES	1 SUMMER HILL
F9	DAVID OWEN DARLEY DAVIES	BRYNFORD STREET
F11	JOSEPH LAWTON DENTON	CROSS STREET
L39	GEORGE EDWARDS	8 BANK PLACE
L40	ROBERT JOHN EDWARDS	8 BANK PLACE
L41	SAMUEL EDWARDS	6 BAGILLT STREET
L42	JOHN EDWARDS	6 RAVEN COURT
L43	THOMAS EDWARDS	4 PRIMROSE HILL
L44	JAMES EGLIN	8 BANK PLACE
L45	JOHN RICHARD EVANS	HIGH STREET
L46	JOHN THOMAS EVANS	5 CHAPEL TERRACE
L47	WILLIAM EDWARD EVANS	2 BRYNFORD TERRACE
L48	JOHN LITTLER EVANS	2 BRYNFORD TERRACE
L49	JOHN PETER EVANS	BRYNFORD TERRACE
L50	JOHN FRANCIS EVANS	2 ROSE HILL
L51	ROBERT EVANS	25 WELL STREET
F12	ROBERT EDWARDS	TY-COCH, PEN-Y-BALL STREET
F15	DAVIS EDWARD EVANS	BLODWEN VILLAS
F16	WILLIAM NOEL EVANS	MOSS BANK
L53	THOMAS FERGUSON	THE HERMITAGE, SUMMERHILL

ID	Name	Address
L54	WILLIAM FERGUSON	THE HERMATAGE, SUMMERHILL
L55	PETER FERGUSON	RED LION YARD
L57	IVOR FOULKES	19 GREENFIELD STREET
L58	MOSES FOULKES	19 GREENFIELD STREET
F17	A H FISHER	BRYNFORD STREET
L59	JOSEPH HENRY GALLAGHER	2 RAVEN COURT
L60	THOMAS GALLAGHER	2 RAVEN COURT
L61	RICHARD GRAHAM	1 PEN-Y-BALL STREET
L62	RICHARD OWEN GRIFFITHS	13 NEW ROAD
L63	THOMAS TUDOR GRIFFITHS	BRYN TEG, WHITFORD STREET
L64	THOMAS PATRICK HAYDEN	OAKFIELD, WHITFORD STREET
L65	MICHAEL HAYDEN	CLAREMONT, WELL STREET
L66	WILLIAM HESSE	WHITFORD STREET
L67	WILLIAM E. HIGGINBOTHAM	4 ROSE HILL
L68	WALTER HILL	POLICE STATION
L69	JAMES HENRY HILL	POLICE STATION
L70	THOMAS HOLMES	WHITFORD STREET
L71	EDWIN HOUGH	10 TOWER GARDENS PLACE
L72	JOHN PRICE HOUGH	10 TOWER GARDENS PLACE
L73	WILLIAM ERNEST HUGHES	VICTORIA SQUARE
L74	JAMES HUGHES	4 LOWER SUMMERHILL
L75	LLEWELLYN HUGHES	1 ROSE HILL
L76	THOMAS HENRY HUGHES	3 ROSE HILL
L77	RICHARD LLOYD HUGHES	8 ROSE HILL
L78	HERBERT HUGHES	36 WHITFORD STREET
L79	ROBERT EVERARD HUGHES	36 WHITFORD STREET
L80	JOHN HERBERT HUGHES	BRYNFORD TERRACE
L81	WILLIAM PRITCHARD HUGHES	UPPER BROGNALLT
L21BRY	THOMAS EDWARD HUGHES	LAUREL COTTAGE PWLL CLAI
L22BRY	ROBERT JOHN HUGHES	GLANLLYN PWLL CLAI
L23BRY	JOHN EDWARD HUGHES	SMITHY GATE PEN-Y-BALL
F19	A T HINSLEY	BRYNFORD ROAD

ID	Name	Address
L83	GEORGE HAROLD JACKSON	CONVENT VIEW, WELL STREET
L84	DAVID GWILYM JACKSON	24 WELL STREET
L85	WILLIAM JACKSON	1 ST WINNIFRED'S TERRACE
L86	CHARLES JOHNSON	KINGS HEAD
L87	CECIL JOHNSON	KINGS HEAD
L88	JAMES JOHNSON	KINGS HEAD
L89	HENRY JOHNSON	KINGS HEAD
L90	LEONARD JONES	1 PANTON PLACE
L91	HERBERT JONES	1 PANTON PLACE
L93	JOHN PETER JONES	9 ABBOTTS TERRACE
L94	ROBERT GRIFFITH JONES	DEE VIEW, BRYNFORD STREET
L95	HARRY BEVAN JONES	1 BAGILLT STREET
L96	EDWARD NORMAN JONES	1 BAGILLT STREET
L97	AQUILA JONES	VRON VIEW, HIGH STREET
L98	DAVID OWEN JONES	MANCHESTER HOUSE, HIGH STREET
L99	THOMAS RICHARD JONES	THE BLACK HORSE INN
L100	WALTER OWEN JONES	4 SEA VIEW TERRACE
L101	CHARLES JONES	4 PEN-Y-BALL STREET
L102	ARTHUR H. THOMAS JONES	VICTORIA COTTAGES
L103	JOHN RICHARD JONES	STRAND COTTAGE
L104	JOHN JONES	27 WELL STREET
L105	JAMES GOMER JONES	19 PEN-Y-BALL STREET
L106	PRYCE MORRIS JONES	46 PEN-Y-BALL STREET
L107	WILLIAM PETER JONES	3 BANK PLACE
L108	JOHN T. JONES	1 DOLPHIN COTTAGES
L109	WILLIAM JONES	8 LOWER BROGNALLT
L110	EDWARD JONES	1 LOWER BROGNALLT
L112	JOHN DAVID JONES	BLUEBELL YARD
L113	JOHN PEARSON JONES	1 BRYNFORD TERRACE
L114	JOHN GWILYM JONES	36 NEW ROAD
L115	HERBERT GLYN JONES	36 NEW ROAD
L116	OWEN THOMAS JONES	36 NEW ROAD

ID	Name	Address
L117	DAVID GRIFFITH JONES	31 WHITFORD STREET
L118	JOHN JONES	32 BRYNFORD STREET
L119	GWILYM JONES	32 BRYNFORD STREET
L120	JOHN OWEN JONES	15 PRIMROSE HILL
L121	WILLIAM EDWARD JONES	1 PRIMROSE HILL
L122	JOHN THOMAS JONES	LOWER SUMMERHILL
L123	DAVID JAMES JONES	LOWER SUMMERHILL
L124	WILLIAM HENRY JONES	5 LOWER SUMMERHILL
L125	ROGER CONELIUS JONES	5 LOWER SUMMERHILL
L126	THOMAS JONES	11 LOWER GARDENS PLACE
L128	GEORGE JONES	5 NEW ROAD
L129	ERNEST D. JONES	ROSE VILLA, ROSE HILL
L24BRY	DANIEL JENKINS	BRYNFORD COTTAGES
L31BRY	JOHN RICHARD JONES	PENLLONGLE COTTAGE
F22	PERCIVAL W. JERVIS	BRYNFORD STREET
F26	E N JONES	4 BANK PLACE
L131	GWILYM KENNEDY	11 BANK PLACE
L132	JAMES LEDSHAM	14 RED HOUSES
L133	JAMES LEDSHAM	14 RED HOUSES
L134	DAVID LITTLER	CROSS GUNS, BAGILLT STREET
L135	THOMAS LLOYD	8 BANK PLACE
L136	NEVILLE OSBOURNE LLOYD	BRYN SIRIOL, PEN-Y-MAES
L137	JASON HERBERT LLOYD	42 PEN-Y-BALL STREET
F28	JOHN E LUKE	PISTYLL COTTAGES
L140	WILLIAM MATHER	TALACRE COTTAGE
L141	JOHN MATTHEWS	22 BAGILLT STREET
L142	ROBERT THOMAS MATTHEWS	21 PEN-Y-BALL STREET
L143	DAVID MCEVILLY	5 SUMMERHILL
L144	FRANCIS MCLOUGHLIN	6 BANK PLACE
L145	JOHN MCNAMARA	ST. DAVID'S TERRACE
L146	JOHN BERTIE MILLINS	HOTEL VICTORIA
L147	ALFRED MONKS	THE NOOK, SUMMERHILL

ID	Name	Address
L148	GEORGE MORRIS	16 PANTON PLACE
L149	WILLIAM NEE	TY-COCH, PEN-Y-BALL STREET
L150	MICHAEL NEE	TY-COCH, PEN-Y-BALL STREET
L151	WILLIAN NEVILLE	CROSSROADS
L152	JAMES NORTON	TAN Y BRYN, BRYNFORD STREET
L153	ALBERT NUTALL	12 PRIMROSE HILL
F4BRY	SAMUEL NEEDHAM	PWLL CLAI
L154	W F OWENS	5 THE GROVE
L42BRY	GEORGE EDWARD OARE	NAID-Y-MARCH
L155	EDWARD JOSEPH PARRY	1 RED HOUSES
L156	JOSEPH PARRY	15 RED HOUSES
L157	EDWARD SAMUEL PARRY	20 BRYNFORD STREET
L158	GEORGE HERDORE PARRY	9 ROSE HILL
L160	GWILYM P. PARRY PHILLIPS	15 PANTON PLACE
L162	EDWARD ASHLEY PIERCE	BOD-ALOW
L163	JOHN PRITCHARD PRICE	3 HUTCHFIELD ROW
L164	EDWARD PRICE	10 ABBOTS TERRACE, PEN-Y-MAES
F30	J H PARRY	RED HOUSES
F31	SAMUEL PULFORD	PERTH-Y-TERYN
L165	DAVID WILLIAM REES	20 GREENFIELD STREET
L166	EDWARD REDFERN	10 PANTON PLACE
L167	LLEWELLYN RICHARDS	MAES WHITFORD
L168	ELFORD HARDING ROBERTS	PENORE, WHITFORD STREET
L169	JOHN ERNEST ROBERTS	25 WELL STREET
L170	JOSEPH LEONARD ROBERTS	25 WELL STREET
L171	JOHN JOSEPH ROBERTS	3 LOWER BROGNAULLT
L172	WILLIAM SAMUEL ROBERTS	7 RED HOUSES
L173	ROBERT THOMAS ROBERTS	17 RED HOUSES
L174	JASON THOMAS ROBERTS	16 TOWER GARDENS PLACE
L175	THOMAS ROBERTS	16 TOWER GARDENS PLACE
L176	EDWIN ROBERTS	17 PRIMROSE HILL
L177	DAVID HENRY ROBERTS	EXCHANGE SHOP, HIGH STREET

ID	Name	Address
L178	SAMUEL ROBERTS	50 PEN-Y-BALL STREET
L179	EDWARD GORDON ROBERTS	5 BAGILLT STREET
F32	ROBERT RAWSON	BRYNFORD STREET
F33	JOHN E. ROBERTS	THE GROVE
L181	JOHN FRANCIS SAUNDERS	31 BRYNFORD STREET
L182	THOMAS ARTHUR SAUNDERS	31 BRYNFORD STREET
L183	BASIL SCHWARZ	WHITFORD STREET
L184	LEONARD SCHWARZ	WHITFORD STREET
L185	GEORGE ARNOLD SCOTCHER	15 HIGH STREET
L186	GODFREY SELLERS	GREYMOUNT, WELL STREET
L187	ERIC SELLERS	GREYMOUNT, WELL STREET
L188	THOMAS WILLIAM SIBEON	AUGHTON HOUSE, BRYNFORD STREET
L189	WILLIAM NEWTON SKELTON	THE GROVE, HOLYWELL
L190	ERNEST FREDRICK SMITH	11 NEW ROAD
L191	JOHN STEALEY	HILLSIDE FARM
L57BRY	DANIEL SMITH	TAN-Y-BRYN PWLL-CLAI
L58BRY	JAMES SPENCER	GATEHOUSE FARM
L192	JOHN WILLIAM THOMAS	WINTER ROW, OFF BRYNFORD STREET
L193	SHEM THOMAS	WINTER ROW, OFF BRYNFORD STREET
L194	JOSEPH THOMAS	12 HIGH STREET
L195	WILLIAM TRUEMAN	9 PRIMROSE HILL
L196	PETER TRUEMAN	9 PRIMROSE HILL
L197	GEORGE JAMES VALE	TOWN HALL
L198	ANDREW WALKER	MOUNT ZEON, REW ROAD
L199	WILLIAM RATHBONE WHITE	2 TROS-Y-MAES VILLAS
L200	PETER WILKES	BAGILLT STREET
L201	JOHN WILKES	20 RED HOUSES
L202	THOMAS EWART WILLIAMS	GROVE COTTAGE
L203	EDWARD NEVILLE WILLIAMS	GROVE COTTAGE
L204	WILLIAM OWEN WILLIAMS	1 ALLEN SQUARE
L205	THOMAS WILLIAMS	4 ALLEN SQUARE
L206	JOHN WILLIAMS	1 ST. WINIFRED'S TERRACE

ID	Name	Address
L207	STEPHEN WILLIAMS	1 ST. WINIFRED'S TERRACE
L208	ISAAC WILLIAMS	FIELD HOUSE
L209	EDWARD WILLIAMS	1 ARGYLE COTTAGES
L210	JOSEPH TOPPING WILLIAMS	DAVIES SQUARE
L212	ROBERT THOMAS WILLIAMS	TROS-Y-MAES
L213	JOHN WILLIAMS	3 TROS-Y-MAES
L214	JOSEPH HENRY WILLIAMS	18 NEW ROAD
L215	ROBERT EDWARD WILLIAMS	16 NEW ROAD
L216	JAMES A. WILLIAMS	16 NEW ROAD
L217	JOSPEH LLEWL. WILLIAMS	ROSE VILLA
L218	NEVILLE W. WILLIAMS	ROSE VILLA
L219	THOMAS WILLIAMS	2 DOLPHIN COTTAGES
L221	ROBERT E. WILLIAMS	19 RED HOUSES
L222	JOHN GRIFFITH WILLIAMS	BOARS HEAD INN
L223	JOHN WILLIAMS	29 WELL STREET
L224	RICHARD WILLIAMS	44 PEN-Y-BALL STREET
L225	JOHN EDWARD WILLIAMS	44 PEN-Y-BALL STREET
L228	JOHN EDWARD WILLIAMS	WHITFORD STREET
L229	WILLIAM DAVID WILLIAMS	CROSS STREET
L230	JOHN ROBERT WILLIAMS	11 PRIMROSE HILL
L232	EDWARD THOMAS WILLIAMS	CHINA HOUSE, BRYNFORD STREET
L234	DAVID THOMAS WINTER	4 PEN-Y-BALL STREET
L235	THOMAS WINTER	12 BANK PLACE
L236	SAMUEL WILSON	BLUE BELL COTTAGES
L237	ROBERT WILSON	BLUE BELL YARD
L239	JAMES WORTHINGTON	15 WHITFORD STREET
L240	JOSEPH WILLIAM WYNNE	6 PRIMROSE HILL
L241	THOMAS WYNNE	WOLVERDENE, COLSHILL STREET
L64BRY	EDWARD W.M. WILLIAMS	PWLL CLAI
L66BRY	WILLIAM E. WILLIAMS	HENBLAS FARM, HENBLAS
F34	LESLIE A. WALLWORTH	WELL STREET
F35	WILLIAM WILLIAMS	THE DOLPHIN INN, WHITFORD STREET

F36	J E WILLIAMS	GRAPES HOUSE, HIGH STREET
F37	J LLEW WILLIAMS	GRAPES HOUSE, HIGH STREET
F38	EDWIN WILLIAMS	TROS-Y-MAES
F39	HUGH OSBOURNE WILLIAMS	TROS-Y-MAES
F40	MESECH WILLIAMS	1 ST. WINIFRED'S TERRACE
F41	WILLIAM WILLIAMS	1 ST. WINIFRED'S TERRACE
L242	ROBERT JOSEPH YARNELL	4 GREENFIELD STREET

It has been a privilege to research the men listed on the Holywell Memorial. I would like the book to finish with a very poignant poem by Vera Brittain who lost her Fiance Roland Leighton, her Brother Edward and close friends Victor Richardson and Jeffrey Thurlow in the War.

Vera Brittain

Perhaps (1916) by Vera Brittain

Perhaps some day the sun will shine again
And I shall see that still the skies are blue
And feel once more I do not live in vain
Although I feel bereft of you

Perhaps the golden meadows at my feet
Will make the sunny hours of Spring seem gay
And I shall find the white May blossom sweet
Though you have passed away

Pehaps the summer woods will shimmer bright
And crimson roses once again be fair
And autumn harvest fields a rich delight
Although you are not there

Perhaps some day I shall not shrink in pain
To see the passing of the dying year
And listen to the Christmas songs again
Although you cannot hear

But though kind time may many joys renew
There is one greatest joy, I shall not know
Again, because my heart for loss of you
Was broken long ago

Sources and Permissions

- WIKI.ORG
- W.F.A. WESTERN FRONT ASSOCIATION
- ENGLISHVERSE.COM
- TUNSTILLSMENBLOGSPTO.COM
- CHRISTOPHER WILLIAMS ART
- HISTORYPOINTS.ORG
- WWW.C.W.G.C.ORG
- WWW.GREATWARFORUM.ORG
- NATIONAL ARCHIVES
- WWW.FLINTSHIREWRMEMORIALS.COM
- PLAYER.BFI.ORG/UK/FREE/FILM
- THE IMPERIAL WAR MUSEUM
- HAWARDEN RECORD OFFICE
- BRIAN TAYLOR - HOLYWELL AND DISTRICT SOCIETY
- PETER MEDCALF
- NICK DENTON
- ROYAL AUSTRAILIAN NAVY
- POEMS IN TRANSLATION
- FINDMYPAST
- FORCES WAR RECORDS
- WELCOME COLLECTION
- WIKIMEDIACOMMONS

Printed in Great Britain
by Amazon